GLASGOW
SMELLS

A Nostalgic Tour
of the City

GLASGOW SMELLS

A Nostalgic Tour
of the City

MICHAEL MEIGHAN

TEMPUS

For Martin, Jim and Stephen
who also experienced those same sights,
sounds and smells.

Frontispiece: Glasgow, courtesy of Janice Mennie (www.mennieprints.co.uk).

First published 2007

Tempus Publishing
Cirencester Road, Chalford,
Stroud, Gloucestershire, GL6 8PE
www.tempus-publishing.com

Tempus Publishing is an imprint of NPI Media Group

Typesetting and origination by NPI Media Group
Printed in Great Britain

ACKNOWLEDGEMENTS

I would like to thank the following people for their help and assistance in compiling this book: first of all, those who illustrated it, particularly Graham MacLennan (graham@cartoon.fsworld. co.uk) for his cartoons and Janice Mennie (www.mennieprints.co.uk) for her paintings as well as Catriona Meighan for the No. 4 Bus. And to Douglas Lillie and John Ross for the Late Andrew Chalmers Lillie's super paintings of Springburn, which he produced when he learned that Springburn was going to be redeveloped, and also for his poem, 'Oor Close'.

I am grateful to David McLaughlin for his photographs of Anderston Cross and Argyle Street. To Peter and Janet Christie for allowing me to copy Dan Ferguson's drawing of Shamrock Street. Also to Scottish Television for the photographs of the *One O'Clock Gang* stars. To The Scottish Council for Development and Industry for photos from the 1953 book, *Scottish Industry*. To Henry Mennie for his 'pissoir' photo. To the wonderful Mitchell Library for photos from their collection.

I would also like to thank the team at Tempus Publishing for their support and feedback.

I am also grateful to all those who read and laughed as well as giving me support, advice and stories. To Graham and Lesley, Janice and Henry, Jim, Martin, Gerald, Angela, Stephen, Chris and Catriona, and especially, to Jill.

Michael Meighan
July 2007

'Wha daur meddle wi' me?'

"*Let our watchword be order, our beacon beauty.*"

INTRODUCTION

There comes a time in life when we wish to review what we are and what we have achieved. Many of us look back to our childhood, to the people and the places that influenced us. Some of us are content to simply remember the pleasure of what gave us joy or what made us cry.

As we get older we sometimes wonder why life is not as certain as it was when we were young; why things are not as simple and straightforward as they were in our childhood. The years seem shorter and the summers do not last as long as when we were children.

As for me, while I like to remember my childhood I also want to write about it. On balance it was a good childhood lived in Glasgow. A childhood moulded in Anderston, Garngad, and Bridgeton and everywhere in the city that was a playground such as you could not find in any Disneyland.

But where to start? As I think about my childhood I realise that what formed the geography of Glasgow could be interpreted by its sounds, its sights but particularly by its smells. Smells of the city and the river, smells of the slums, smells of the school and the church and the smells of Glasgow in general. I thought that one way to explore my past was by delving into the city through the way it used to smell as well as remembering the sights and the sounds.

And how do you describe a smell? Come with me on a journey through Glasgow in the fifties and sixties and see if you can't get a whiff of life then for the Glaswegian...

The Tram

Unlike the silent glide of the trolleybus you can hear the tram from a long way off. Clanking on the joints or screeching its way round a steel bend. Or rattling over a crossing, never minding the other traffic but ploughing on with certainty of place and power.

At night you can see it too, wobbling over the crossings, blue-white stars shooting like a Guy Fawkes Night sparkler, emerging from the tenement tunnels and settling to a stop. 'We're only going to Glesga Cross.' 'Aye ok, I'll walk the rest.'

You climb into the tram past the driver and right away you get the smells. How can you smell electricity? Well, you could on a Glasgow tram. They say it's the smell of ozone but quite definitely you can smell the slight burn, the acrid tinge as the contacts were made and the tram moved off – not unpleasant, not an odour, just a smell that belongs there and nowhere else.

And then the smell of leather polished by a million bums. Leather that has been shined by boiler suits from Clydebank and army uniforms, apprentices and office girls, sliding in and out. Women in curlers on their way to the Barraland.

Your hand finds the polished steel poles and handles and you slide into your seat. If you are lucky and it is quiet you can go up top and lean out of the front window. The thought of this on a sunny day as the tram speeds along Argyle Street through the bustle of a Saturday morning.

I didn't smoke then but the thought of the brass match strikers on the back of the seats brings back the memories of Bogie Roll and Cut Plug and the pervading smell of tobacco. Not the caustic smell of cigarette and butt but the pleasant odour of pipe tobacco cut and rolled, packed and smoked and tamped out on the rutted wooden floor.

I can taste the pipe tobacco. I can even taste the tram ticket as I chew it. I can still touch the green and brown leather, scrape my finger along the brass striker, slide my hand on the steel and hurt my hand on the high leather straps as I pretend a tallness I don't yet have.

And at no time is there such a distillation and compress of smell as on an evening when it pours like cats and dogs and smell, odour, people, tram and workplace become as one. Then you get the smell of Glasgow, from the sweat of honest work, the beery smell of a Friday night, the tenement smell, escaping the rain at all costs, and pushing together in one moving Glasgow electric tenement.

Glasgow Cross

There was nowhere in Glasgow where the smell enveloped you as it did at Glasgow Cross. At that interchange of roads and cultures the smells came in great swathes of gaseous envelopes and if you had your eyes closed you could tell almost exactly where you were.

To the south of the Cross, at Victoria Bridge, was the Fish Market with its wet smell. Fresh fish, whelk, prawns, supplemented by salmon, cod roes and other mysteries of the seas.

The rough cries, the wet smells, the fish smell, the cold smell of ice and acrid waste. The smell of poultry, rows of hanging birds, plucked and ready, soft hen eggs. The smell of freshness turning sour.

The blue coats, white rubber aprons and welly boots of the fish ladies, their hoses washing down the pavements, the offal floating down the bloody gutters. All gone now for better, more hygienic times, except for some remnants of traders in Stockwell Street and around.

'Kid on you're daft and ye'll get a hurl for nothing.'

To the east where, on Saturdays and Sundays the crowds streamed to the Barras along Gallowgate and London Road. Here, near Shipka Pass, you could buy hot roasted chestnuts and see an escapologist setting up shop in the road, being locked into and then getting out of thick chains. In Gallowgate the shop selling salty-smelling boiled whelks for which you also got a little pin to pull the whelk out of its little grey shell.

To the north, the Cheese Market, now a concert hall. You could walk into the market, into the racks of maturing, dullish yellow and cream cheeses, some the size of small barrels. Barrels of butter. The tangy smell of ancient cheeses. Cheeses before the present process which produces yellow rubber. Big yellow slices of strong Scottish cheddar on thick slices of a Glasgow loaf. Lovely!

Also to the north were the stables for the Glasgow police horses and if I went by to my granny's I could see them parading and practicing in Bell Street, maybe before setting off to police Hampden or Parkhead football grounds. As the enormous horses stomped around getting into line, guided by their riders in large black capes, there would gather monumental mounds of steaming dung which would be left to be cleared up by the stable hands.

And near the Fish Market, Paddy's Market – partly underneath the railway arches but spilling out wherever it could onto lane and pavement and brokie. Paddy's Market with its smell of old clothes, wet brick and pea brae. Pea brae was peas cooked in vinegar, which was delicious. Paddy's Market was so called because many of the original dealers in the 1820s were Irish.

And particularly Paterson's Camp Coffee. To this day I do not know exactly where the factory was. The memories that I have of walking from Anderston to Bridgeton along Argyle Street to see granny on a Sunday. As we approached Glasgow Cross, dad and I, noses filled with the most concentrated smell and taste of coffee and chicory. Camp was a mixture of coffee and chicory. Camp Coffee is still made, now by a multinational company, but then by Paterson's in Glasgow.

Put these smells together with the smell of trolley bus, tram, and the sulphurous smoke from the underground railway coming up the shaft at the Tolbooth church. The stench of petrol from inefficient ex-army lorries and the Saturday crowds coming from or going to a match at Parkhead, or to the Barras, with their fish suppers and beery smell. I swear I can still smell it as I walk now across Glasgow Cross on a quieter day than then.

And for information, you might like to know that when the cast-iron panels round the back of the Glasgow Cross Caledonian Railway station were dismantled, they were re-erected on St Vincent Place.

The cast-iron panels from the back of the Glasgow Cross Caledonian railway station, which were re-erected on St Vincent Place.

Smells on North Street

Well, it wasn't really a very smelly street but it was my street and I thought that it was full of smells and few of them unpleasant. I would choose North Street for its length and its interest as well as its smells and because I was born there, or at least raised there.

When you got to the foot of our stairs and emerged onto North Street what you saw was a billboard set in a 'brokie'. I can still see the BOAC (British Overseas Airways Corporation) poster for some exotic faraway place that we could not aspire to, and I remember that the name of the company owning the billboard was on a sign underneath – More O'Ferrall. Apparently my memory is prodigious and that is also one reason I am writing this book – to get it all down before it fades.

We lived above Davy Ireland's tobacconists. Inside the shop was darkish, lit by one or two bulbs. But it was a big square room and Davy, whom I can remember only vaguely, would be talking to his cronies, Cutting Bogie Roll or Bulwark Cut Plug and weighing it on little brass scales before putting it into a 'poke', a twist of newspaper.

I would be in the shop for a caramel dainty, my Beezer or 'ginger'. On the counter would be *The Evening Citizen*, *The People's Friend* and *Ireland's Own*. I can smell the firewood in bundles. The thick tobacco smoke, the raw tobacco and the smell of newsprint. I swear that it had a smell back then.

I can remember a big glass cabinet along the wall in which there were such exotic pieces of hardware as a shiny metal oval, combined tea and sugar tins, tea tins with metal loop handles,

'*The Green Citizen*' on a Saturday with the football results.

gas mantles, double-ended baby feeding bottles, baby-bottle teats on cardboard and Bronco or San Izal toilet rolls: in fact, everything for everybody up the next close.

Then Danny's Fish and Chip Shop, a scrubbed and spotless high, plain wood counter and absolutely nothing else for sale except fish and chips or pie and chips. I don't even remember pickled onions and certainly not gherkins. None of your new-fangled deep-fried Mars Bars or pizza suppers. Just quality haddock straight from Aberdeen and fresh-cut chips covered in crisp salt and sharp-smelling vinegar. None of yer salt and sauce? Here, boy. What could be better?

I remember a row of two-storey houses with stairs in the back closes. These were some of the original village houses in Anderston before the tenements came. They were to be knocked down before we left. Some of them were derelict but I do remember them being used, one as an illegal betting shop.

When I was young, betting was illegal, but many people did it. Runners would take bets to a bookmaker and then make a payout if you were lucky. I think my dad may have bet occasionally! Anyway there was also an illegal bookmaker in the row of houses and every so often you would hear the sound of the Black Maria's bells and the illegal betting shop would be raided and the punters herded into the van. A Black Maria was a police van which was used on raids, so called because they were black but named after Maria Lee, a very large lady who helped the constables of Boston, Massachusetts in the 1830s when they needed to escort drunks to the cells. Another version that I have heard was that Maria was a lady who was condemned to death and only wore black throughout her trial.

Across the road was the corner where I got the autographs of the two most famous footballers in the world! Real Madrid were playing Eintracht Frankfurt at Hampden in the finals of the European Cup and some of them had come to St Pat's for Mass. I believe they were staying at the Central Hotel. As they walked down North Street they were spotted and I ran up the stairs to get my autograph book, the book with the green marbled surface and yellow letters that spelled 'Autographs' diagonally across the front.

For many years I kept that book with the autographs of Alfred di Stephano and Ferenc Puskas. During the match on 18 May 1960 the pair scored seven goals, beating Eintracht by 7-3 and retaining the European Cup. Real Madrid had previously beaten Rangers 12-4 on aggregate in the semi-final.

This match was described by the late great Jimmy Johnstone: 'The match remained the biggest single influence on my career. It was like a fantasy staged in heaven. I had never seen football like it, nor would I ever again. I'll recite the names of that Madrid forward line till the day I die.'

Incidentally, the autograph book also had such local stars as Larry Marshall and Johnnie Beattie. I don't know what happened to it but I have a feeling that it will turn up sometime.

Then up the road past the cemetery at which gate I found a poor tramp dead. North Street could be very quiet. On that day it was empty as a pal and I came down the hill and there, in front of the cemetery gates, was the body of a man, on his back. We gazed at him for what seemed like ages and eventually assumed he was dead. We ran up the road to the police box. I don't particularly remember any horror about it but I do remember that he was the first person I ever saw dead outside a coffin. I remember that he was wearing an old suit and an old worn-out tweed coat and I assumed that he was a tramp as we had read about them in books.

Then up to Greig's wool warehouse. Here was a multi-storey stable converted into a warehouse. In the fifties, the need for livery stables was drawing to a close and they were being used for other purposes, in this case, a company that exported wool. I remember the heavy, oily, musty, sheepy smell of wool baled in sacking, particularly in the summer. It was the kind of solid smell that made you thirsty because of its dryness. But they kept their bin at the front door and you could always be guaranteed to find lots of stamps from Pakistan with the scimitar and stars. Sometimes they came from other areas too.

You can see the warehouse in the photograph on the next page. In front of it is the cemetery where remains were being disinterred prior to being sent for reburial. They had put boards up so that the public couldn't see but reckoned without my trusty Brownie 127 and me on the roof of our building.

The cemetery was being deconsecrated to allow the building of the new motorway and what you can see on the next page is where the approach to the Kingston Bridge is now. Even then, in what I think was 1962 or 1963, the first modern office blocks were up.

The remains within the cemetery were re-interred at Linn Park in Glasgow. I know this because of my research. I have a friend from Australia who visited Glasgow one day. He told me that he had been looking for the graveyard in which his grandmother, a Sutherland from Sutherland, had been buried. He explained where he had been told it was but was unable to find it. With some research I had found that this was the only graveyard that had been moved so she must have been buried there. It's a small world I suppose!

And just beyond here on the same side was the close from where they took the man who had died of gas poisoning. These days, our 'natural' gas comes from wells drilled in the North Sea. It differs from the old 'town gas' in that it has no smell and I believe that a smell has to be added to it to alert us if there is an escape. The old town gas certainly had a smell. This was made in huge 'retorts' which cooked coal to produce both gas and coke as a by-product.

Town gas had a bitter, oily, acrid smell and taste and you knew it right away. You would know in any town where the gas works was by its huge round gasometer but mainly by its smell. You couldn't mistake the stench and that's what makes the deaths so desperate. The expression 'I'll stick my head in the gas oven' was well known and used not only by those in complete despair but as an alternative to Anadin, I suppose, for relieving the pressure.

Unfortunately, it was also an easy way of committing suicide as the gas would act quickly in a confined tenement room, particularly if doors were sealed with towels or paper. I had not seen the effects but one day while walking down North Street, I saw the white St Andrew's ambulance parked outside a close just beside the police box opposite the church. The ambulancemen in their dark uniforms came out with this man on a brown canvas stretcher covered with a grey blanket. They had not covered his face. I did not know him and don't know if I would have recognised him anyway as his face was covered with what looked like puffy grey blobs. It was quite clear he was dead and the smell of gas still lifted from his body as he was put into the ambulance and taken away. You don't sleep well after something like that and you wonder whether it was an accident and, if not, what would cause someone to want to do that.

What I remember most was his greyness, the grey sombreness of the ambulancemen and the onlookers and the fact that it was overall a very, very grey day.

The disinterring
of North Street
Cemetery, *c.* 1962.

From our roof
to the 'Greek'
Thomson church
(right).

Then up by the big brokie, which was where the biggest Guy Fawkes bonfire always was. The roasting heat of the bonfire with the smell of burning timber mostly salvaged from derelict buildings and hoarded.

Across the road was St Patrick's Catholic church and girl's school and at the other side of William Street was the strangest shop from out of the Middle Ages. In a door straight off the pavement was a big room down a small flight of steps where sat four or five women chopping firewood, some with a machine that came down on the wood, splitting it into pieces. You could stop here and pass the time of day with them before wandering further up. It was a dark, musty place smelling of wood, resin and cigarette smoke, all captured within the room which had only the front door for ventilation.

And next door, McFall's Dairy for whom I sometimes delivered milk. Big white-haired Charlie McFall behind the counter where you could get the smell of cheese and milk and ham rolls.

Across St Vincent Street, exactly where I stood to see the Queen and Prince Philip immediately after the Coronation. Me with my little Union Jack. There was the St Andrew's ambulance depot where I did my first aid badge. Then The Office pub. 'I've been to The Office, dear!'

Then Charing Cross railway station. Through the door and down the stairs with the train and steam smells coming up to meet you as the ticket man issued you your little card ticket for the two stops to school. I remember that door well as there was for a long time inside it a wanted poster for the 'Great Train Robbers'.

On up and you passed the famous Hut pub and opposite was the Mitchell Library where I read many a copy of *The Sunday Post* with Oor Wullie and the Broons. They were kept then in enormous musty volumes of about a year at a time. And you had to order these and get them from a window before taking them to a big desk to read. You could read a whole year of wartime cartoons in one go.

It's funny how all Glasgow libraries smelled the same. The Mitchell smelled of polish, books and particularly linoleum polish. I think that they were proud of their floors and I remember signs up barring women from wearing stiletto heels. Out of the library and on up the street to Sauchiehall Street and then you could go on beyond to the park but that's another story…

Anderston

I also have to take a bit of a short walk round Anderston, generally because the more I think of the smells, the more they come back to me. If we start off from my close and turn round the corner by the Queens Arms into Argyle Street, across the road is The Gaiety Bar which my Uncle Jimmy ran and where my father worked at nights occasionally.

When I was in the Scouts we had to do Bob-a-Job. I don't think that this exists any more for safety reasons but then we raised money for the Scouts by asking everyone and anyone if we could do a job for them. My first port of call was The Gaiety, where my uncle would let me sweep out the whitewashed cellar and stamp the returnable beer bottles. I loved the smell down there. It was cool and dank with the wooden barrels of McEwan's lined up on a stone plinth, the barrels of Guinness waiting. Crates of McEwan's in wooden cases. You could smell the sweetness and the bitterness of the beer mixed with the other cellar smells.

It was great when the draymen came. These were the brewery men with their lorry and great big barrels of beer. They had a big sacking pad on which they dropped the barrels: two men caught them together, and one would roll the barrel to the opened cellar doors set flush in the pavement. They would then drop the barrel down the hole onto another pad. It would then be

Above left: Our house is right in the middle.

Below: Hill 60 at Kelvingrove Park.

Glasgow tenements.

rolled off with a clunk before being lifted onto its plinth. Of course we would be shooed out of the way while this was going on. But watching it reminds me of just some of the traditional activities that you would see as being par for the course as you walked along.

A word about my Uncle Jimmy, by way of apology: I was probably a very impressionable child when I was young and easily manipulated. Anyway, my uncle Jimmy was never fat. He was portly and very easy-going and likeable. It happened that one day he was standing for some reason at the corner of Anthony Street and Argyle Street as me and a chum came along. Now *The Topper* was a favourite comic then and in it was Big Fat Boko who I think was some sort of a comic king. Well, I think I was persuaded to peek round the corner and shout to my uncle: 'Hello Big Fat Boko.' 'I'll Big Fat Boko you,' was the swift retort. I swear he chased me round Anderston for a good half hour through the lanes, closes and back courts before I lost him at the big railings behind our house. It was only because these railings were a good ten-feet high that I survived.

Anyway, back to Argyle Street and down towards Anderston Cross where there was a large traffic island at the junction of Argyle Street, Stobcross Street, Washington Street and Bishop Street. Public toilets were in the middle of the island which was fair bustling. It had the toilets, a public phone box with buttons A and B, a police box and seats. You would wonder why someone thought that it was a good idea to put public toilets underground because in many cases that was where they were. I'm not entirely sure, but I think the only ones left like this are in St Vincent Place and in Cathedral Square. However, I'm very happy to be corrected.

Public toilets, located in Cathedral Square.

With the best will in the world it must have been difficult to keep the toilets clean. The pipes were copper and the smell of Brasso mixed with the acrid smell of the dank pits that they were. Some of these were architecturally delightful like those under the Central Station and you can see one in Aberdeen's Union Street where they still have the cast-iron cisterns with glass panels so you can watch them emptying and filling up with water. I was told once that they used to have goldfish in those tanks but I'm not that gullible. Even if they did they probably charged entry to see them, being Aberdeen. And they probably weren't goldfish but haddocks!

Talking of charging, if you really did have to go underground then you would be charged an old penny for it and you would drop the penny in a brass mechanism on the door and this then opened to let you into the 'stall'. Thus giving rise to the expression (from Aberdeen): 'Here I sit, broken-hearted, paid a penny and only farted!'

And while we are on the subject of toilets, there were other types. I am not sure if there were many examples of the 'pissoir' but there was certainly one of the cast-iron variety at Glasgow Cross. Rather than describe it, I subsequently was amazed to find this perfectly preserved specimen behind the Ferintosh Free church on the Black Isle where I used to stay. To clarify – I stayed in a house beside, not in the pissoir or in the church! Many of these pissoirs were made at the Saracen Ironworks in Possilpark.

At the docks, built into the walls of the dockside warehouses were strange toilets with a narrow brick door and little windows like a cell. If you went into these, all it was was a long cast iron tray like a feeding trough and cast-iron separators on the wall. I wasn't supposed to go into these exclusive toilets because above them they had a sign saying: 'Lascars Only', a 'lascar' being the name used then for the foreign seamen that you would see around Anderston and the docks.

Back to Anderston Cross. Besides bus and tram stops, 'All cars stop here', the island had a 'bundy'. Now, a bundy was a time clock set in a green metal cabinet either fixed to a wall or, as at the Cross, set on a metal stand. The purpose was to allow the tram drivers or conductors to punch their time cards, presumably to monitor their hours by 'clocking' in or out, as in most factories at that time.

Well, one day my younger brother, Stephen, had been late for school and was on his last warning. He was on a bus stuck at the traffic lights at High Street while he was heading along Duke Street to

Right: Saracen Ironworks' pissoir.

Overleaf: From Anderston Cross up Argyle Street.

'The Mungo'. He was obviously showing some agitation and the conductor asked him if he was all right. 'No' he said and explained that he was on his last warning and was about to have to accept the physically painful consequences of it, the Lochgelly being at the forefront of torture at that time.

Anyway, the conductor took pity on him, and producing his bundy card and a stubby pencil, tore the card in half and anointed it with the words: 'Dear Teacher, Stephen was late at school because the bus was late, signed ....' On entering the school he clutched this last straw to his chest and made his way to class through the silent corridors. He entered the class to be greeted with, 'Well, Meighan, this is it, I think: what's your excuse?'

Stephen produced the bundy card, which was eyed suspiciously and produced a slow shake of the teacher's head and then an exasperated sigh. 'Meighan', he said, 'you will go far. Sit down son.' Stephen still has the card. He has gone far. To Kuala Lumpur, as a matter of fact.

You will have heard of Onion Johnnies, the cliché of the Frenchman in his beret with his ropes of onions hanging over the front of his bike. Well, I swear that we had them in Anderston: each year they would come and I remember them in a shop next to Thompson's Newsagents at Anderston Cross. The little shop would be awash with straw as they prepared the ropes of onions to fasten all over their bikes in ropes to take round the doors. I swear also that they wore hooped fishermen's jerseys and black berets.

Also at the corner of Argyle Street and Heddle Place was a soup kitchen which catered for down-and-outs mostly I think. You could look in and see rows of scrubbed white tables like something from a cowboy film. What I remember most about it was the smell of scrambled-egg rolls. While they may or may not have provided such luxuries, it is still one of the most abiding smells of Anderston Cross to me.

Well, that and the cooperage from where smoke and steam emerged constantly, along with noises of the banging, scraping and ringing of the manufacture of oak casks for the storage and maturation of Scotch whisky. I now work in the distilling industry and I am lucky enough to visit some of the existing cooperages. Little has changed, and I only need to walk into the Invergordon Cooperage to be transported back to Anderston Cross and the Clyde Cooperage. Incidentally, the Clyde Cooperage Co. was the basis of what is now the Edrington Group, based where 'The Good Year' used to be, in Clydebank.

At the corner of Bishop Street was Green's Ladies Hairdresser. It was very well known and I well remember going in there with my mother. I remember that there was a procedure then called 'singeing'. I was never sure what hair was being singed and I was too scared to ask. So I still don't know, but I do remember the awful smell of burnt hair among the usual smells of shampoo and lady stuff.

At Anderston Cross

He came round from Washington Street, stooped, the parcel clenched between two hands, pointing forwards. I vaguely saw him as I passed on by and I knew the contents of the brown paper parcel. It was not vinegar or posh whisky. It was not lemonade but cheap wine, cheap sherry wine.

For he had the greasy grey overcoat of the down-and-out, the doubt seeker on the pavement of life; in his hands the red wine. But he stumbled. I saw him from the corner of my eye as he missed his footing on the pavement, all his concentration on the protection of the bottle. His foot turned on the edge of the pavement, unbalanced like a boxer. His hands thrown skywards, his feet splayed, his coat wide and flapping and the bottle describing a tumbling brown arc in the morning light to fall and crash against the granite cobbles. The short pause of shock followed by realisation and then a grasping of paper, glass and wine that flowed between his fingers, lifting the bloody mass to his face to suck the last drops of wine as it merged into a mess of soggy blood, wine and paper.

The wrenching cry and throwing into the road with fury that sad mass and, uncertainly turning, sobbing, fingers and cuffs dripping, and then him disappearing off down Stobcross Street. Many a time I have thought of him.

On the other hand another Glaswegian had bought a half-bottle of Bells and put it into his back pocket. While coming down the stairs, he stumbled and fell on his arse. Putting his hand to his backside he said, 'Oh ma Goad, ah hope that's blood.'

The Subway

There is hardly anyone of my era from Glasgow who is not proud of 'the Subway', as we called it. It is the first thing we wanted to show visitors. This toytown train in its little tunnels. It has a smell of its own. A moist, musty, funereal odour which gets stronger as you descend the steps and even stronger when the blast of air is pushed out of the tunnel in front of the train.

I don't know if it is unique but once you have visited the great subway systems of London and Paris, our tiddly one seems like an embarrassment in comparison. It is small and goes round and round the city on an 'inner circle' and an 'outer circle', probably why it is now known as 'The

Clockwork Orange'. It was named in the era of that famous film at a time when the subway was renovated and the carriages replaced and repainted an orange colour.

It is the old subway that is most vivid to me. The smell is still there but not as strong as it once was when there was more water seeping into the tunnel and when the trains were powered with old tram engines. The trains were famous for their antiquity, their funny little lights, their wooden construction and sliding metal gates like they used to have in shops. As was the whole structure of the tunnels, the dull green station with the single central platform and its enormous metal clock.

It is said that the Glasgow Corporation built the trams themselves when they couldn't get anyone else to do it for such small tunnels. They used the same techniques and materials that they did for the trams but the underground trains outlived the trams by many years.

Round and round the circle I would go on one ticket, particularly on a Sunday, when no one would bother you. You could get out at mysterious faraway places like Cessnock and Cowcaddens. You could do a circuit from St Enoch's, get off at Kinning Park and get the ferry back to Anderston. And at every stage, that all-pervading smell of damp.

One thing I remember in particular, and all credit to the men and women of the underground, for it was that they were a breed apart and proud of it. The drivers and conductors were resplendent and even elegant in their green uniforms with their polished brass buttons.

Some years ago I visited the North of England Industrial Museum at Beamish and there, like a fish out of water, was a Glasgow underground train. It looked so ineffective there almost on its side that I wondered whether the visitors would be aware of the hundreds of thousands of miles that it had travelled beneath Glasgow.

While we are on enterprising Glasgow, I wonder how it ever got that reputation, as Glaswegians are the most dilatory people I know, in general – not casting any aspersions and meaning no one in particular, but where did these expressions come from?

'It's six and half a dozen.'
'We'll see how it goes.'
'It's up to yirsel.'
'Let's play it by ear.'
'It's aw wan.'
'I'm easy-osie!' (All meaning: 'Ah cannae be arsed!')

Wee Janet going 'Doon the Water'.

The River Clyde

'And from Glasgow to Greenock, in towns on each side, the hammer's ding-dong is the song of the Clyde.' The smell of the upper Clyde in the 1950s was dank, a pervasive odour of rotting material, one with which I was to become very familiar with given my nearness to it, living as I did at Anderston Cross, not a mile away from the Cheapside Street ferry.

My father was a great explorer of the city and, by pram he pushed us, and then, walking as we got older, we explored the docks and the Broomielaw. At that time, the Irish and Island boats came all the way up the Clyde to put in at berths from the Finnieston Crane to the Jamaica Bridge. And mixed with the raw pungency of the river, there was the smell of cow dung. Many's the time we would use the gangways for the Irish boats as seesaws as we walked along the Broomielaw.

In the 1950s the Clyde was a fever of activity and all around were smells: the acrid smell of welding and riveting at Harland and Wolff's and many engineering workshops building, fitting out or servicing the ships, great and small; the dry, musty smell of grain at the various mills and the great grain elevators at Partick; the all-pervading smell of whisky from the great bonds; Buchanan's Black and White and the ill-fated Arbuckle Smith bond which was to disappear so tragically in the great Cheapside Street fire.

There was also the smell of Clydesdale horses; the smell of steam and oil from shunters servicing the docks; the cooperages, now long gone from the Clyde but then essential to the supply of barrels for beer and whisky.

What a time we had on the Clyde! There were several pleasures but the best of all were 'The Bumps'. In those days of high and heavy industry, thousands of workers would cross and re-cross the river on the little steam or diesel ferries which would go from steps to steps on either side. What joy there was from mingling with the workmen and being first off the ferry as it bumped up the steps on either side, then waiting to go back again until the skipper got fed up with us: 'Away ye wee buggers till I get my boot to you.' But there was rarely any malice to the threat.

And now I remember one of my first experiences of sailing along the Clyde in the days when paddle steamers left from the Broomielaw to sail 'Doon the Water' to Dunoon, Ireland and other places all along the way, from Govan and right down the Clyde.

My father, mother and brothers and I would line up with full suitcases and prams to be helped up the gangplank at the Broomielaw on to the paddle steamer, which was a new experience, wonder and playground to a child. Just imagine, you could wander the ship, looking over the side to the great paddle wheels churning the black river water, or down to the engines, seeing the pistons working away, and drawing in the heavy, hot smell of diesel oil, wondering at the speed and power of the gleaming pistons and seeing the engineers wandering up and down with their rags and cans, oiling and looking important.

The bar with its fill of Glasgow men making the most of their first day on holiday; the smoky 'buffet' with its heady smell of Guinness and cigarette and pipe tobacco. And of course the toilets with their sticky floors and constant smell of vomit and urine, sometimes with their long-term residents holding on where they could, faces green.

And looking over the stern watching as the sun goes down on Glasgow, passing the tenements, the cranes, the ferries crossing and re-crossing. The lines of ships moving in or out to their worldwide destinations. And then, beginning to see fields: passing the Dumbarton Rock and crossing the bar, smelling the brackish sea, a wondrous wide smell to accompany the whirling seagulls as we sailed on to a holiday at Inellan and new sea and country smells.

There are two strange buildings opposite one another on the Clyde, at Finnieston. One of them, on the north side known as The Rotunda, now houses a restaurant and sits amidst the buildings of the New Clyde, the Glasgow Hilton and the Scottish Exhibition and Conference Centre.

But what is less well known is that these two buildings are at either side end of a famous tunnel which only closed to traffic in the 1980s as a foot tunnel and had previously been a road tunnel with horses and carts, lorries and cars going down on huge lifts and through a tunnel to emerge at either end.

Here is The North Rotunda in the background with the Finnieston crane loading a locomotive onto a ship.

While I did not pass through the vehicle tunnel myself, my father had, and he was able to explain to me how the lifts worked. From a very early age I remember entering the tunnel and being able to look over the barriers down to where the lifts used to go, under a vast glass dome. Besides the smell of stagnant water the most memorable thing in my mind was the constant dripping of water because even in the 1950s and '60s the tunnel was rapidly deteriorating. One of the reasons it was kept open was because of the major water main which ran through the pedestrian tunnel.

And the tunnel itself was the spookiest place in Glasgow. You would go through the entrance and were immediately in the dome and down three or four flights of creaky old wooden stairs before you entered the tunnel proper, which disappeared downwards, and you would look into a dank void lit only sparingly by bulbs at a great distance apart.

I also remember being particularly scared going through the tunnel on my own when someone from the other side would emerge out of the gloom like a phantom. Permeating my memory is the smell of the tunnel, a combination of river, decaying brick and mortar.

The Baby Boomers go to School

Oor wee school's the best wee school
the best wee school in Glesga
The only thing that's wrang wi it
is the baldy-heided maister
He goes tae the pub on a Saturday night
he goes tae church on Sunday
And prays for god tae gie him strength
tae belt the weans on Monday.

City Public Junior Secondary, 1962, with the feared Jimmy 'stand by your beds' Meighan.

The sense of smell is greatly under-rated. Many years after an event, a time or a place, we are brought back to it through a chance odour, fragrance or whiff. This is so true of schooldays. Whether we liked or loathed school, it must be admitted by every ex-pupil that smell plays a large part in memories.

Probably the earliest and most prominent memories are of stale milk. We lived in a time of free school milk when every child received a third of a pint of milk in a little bottle, given out at the morning break. These crates were not collected until much later and, particularly on hot days, the dregs began to smell – a very recognisable but not totally unpleasant sour smell.

The particular memories are of hot summer days in primary school. I went to St Patrick's primary school in Bishop Street, Anderston, Glasgow, a school now long gone, replaced by what is now the Marriot Hotel.

St Patrick's was in the middle of a mixed industrial, commercial and tenement area and particularly on a hot, still day the sounds and smells of the area would waft through the windows. On one side was a small foundry and the smell of molten metal would meet us in the canteen where it would be mixed with the smell of tatties and mince, lentil soup or school cabbage.

There was a large mill in Washington Street where you could go and see the corn or grain being emptied into chutes for processing. This produced a sweet, dusty smell which I was able to identify immediately when I started work in distilleries.

And of course there were the normal smells of school in the fifties. No high technology then. The smell of chalk is so memorable. Chalk in a wide variety of colours. I remember that some teachers could be real artists with the chalk on the large blackboards. Sometimes, the lesson being over, you were asked to clean the board. If it was a particularly hot day and there was lots of chalk on the board, the dust created by removing it would just about choke you.

The famous *Carrick* on the Broomielaw at Victoria Bridge.

Being a Catholic school, religion was extremely important and a pervading smell was that of flowers, which I must admit helped to temper the smell of little boys! At all times of the year there would be a variety of flowers on little altars set up in classrooms. In May, at the Feast of Mary the Mother of Christ, church and school would combine in procession to honour Mary with hymns and lilies, carnations, ferns and others. I particularly remember the smell of wet flowers as they were being arranged around the statues of Mary to be carried from church to school.

One abiding memory was of the headmaster, Brother John Victor, a much-loved Marist Brother. (Our school was run by the Marist Order and was an all-boys school). I remember particularly the smell of his Gold Flake cigarettes. He was a chain smoker and seemed to be able to hold a cigarette in his mouth while the ash got longer until it finally fell off in large dollops down his cassock or over the desk, which during the day became covered in ash and smoke filled the room. Those were in the days when there was no regulation and smoking was more acceptable. Quite often he would send me to the newsagent for twenty Gold Flakes, telling me that I should just say they were for Brother John. Brother John died before his time, unfortunately but not surprisingly of cancer.

On to secondary school in Townhead where the smells were again different: the particular foul smell of the Forth and Clyde Canal, which was being dredged at that time to make way for a new motorway. The short-sightedness of this is all too evident now that the canal has reopened and is promised to rejuvenate whole areas of the central belt.

At that time it was a decaying dump for anything including, if I remember rightly, cars, bikes, guns, all brought to the light of day as the water drained away. The stench of the years of accumulated detritus was something else. I remember one particular story about those days, probably around 1963 at the Port Dundas basin of the Grand Union Canal. There were two Second World War E-boats berthed in the basin. Only recently, I happened to visit, as part of my work, the White Horse grain distillery beside the basin. In the office where I was working I happened to mention to one of the long-term workers there that there used to be two E-boats berthed there. 'So there were,' he said. 'And they are still there – they finally rotted away and sank years ago. What a memory you have boy!'

Townhead is the centre of old Glasgow and when I think back what a historian's joy it was, not that school made history in the least interesting then. There was the Gothic Glasgow Cathedral into which schoolboys were generally not allowed and being Catholic and it a Church of Scotland cathedral we probably thought it was a sin to be there anyway – although it was originally Catholic before the Reformation so what the hell! But occasionally we could get in. It was a place of awe and respect. I can still remember the musty church smell which I thought then must have come from all the dead bodies in the many tombs.

The bell, the bell, the b-i-ell
Tell the teacher tae go tae hell.

While we are on the subject of education, I remember a story told to me by a boss of mine, Bessie Bell, whose father had been stationmaster at Old Kilpatrick (I put that in because I know that Bessie was very proud of the fact). Anyway, she told the story of the teacher with the star pupil at mathematics. On suggesting to her mother that she go on to study maths, the mother replied: 'Whit dis she want maths fir? The only maths she needs is how tae make a half pun o' mince dae seven!'

Also on the communication skills of the Glaswegian, I remember interviewing a Southside lad for a construction job in Aberdeen. I sat him down and said: 'Comfy?' 'Aye', he said, 'Glesga.'

I overheard two Glaswegian oil workers in the Lower Deck bar, part of the Scrabster Hotel, Caithness. They were arguing about the Italian offshore installation manager (OIM) on their oil rig in the North Sea. They felt that he was rather an interfering continental and poked his nose in where it wasn't wanted. 'Whit's the Latin for spanner anyway?' asked one.

'They probably went tae wan o' they schools that were awfy good because they were approved by the Government.'

One teacher from Kelvinside was quizzing the pupils on where they had been for their holidays. After she had received their responses, which included Dunoon, Arbroath, Girvan and Aberdeen, wee Johnny asked her where she had been on holiday. 'Ostend' she said. So they did!

Being tackled by his teacher on the son being a bit cheeky, the mother replied, 'Ah know. He's an impotent wee bugger he is.' I wonder if he ever actually fathered any children?

I am not going to start on the old battle with Edinburgh except when it insults our intelligence. Recently I went into an antiquarian bookshop in Edinburgh, where the antiquarian was sitting behind his desk. 'Hello,' I said, 'do you keep any books about Glasgow?' He looked at me, and with a straight face said, 'No. We only sell books for people that can read.' If I wasn't such a nice person I would tell Glaswegians where he was so they could go over there and batter in his melt!

Actually, he was quite funny. I asked him if he bought books and he said, 'No. We steal them from old ladies'. On you go boys. First left over the Water of Leith. Gie him a Glasgow kiss for me!

Tell tale tit, yer mammy canny knit,
yer daddy cannie go tae bed
withoot a dummy tit.

I was one of those very unfortunate young men who happened to have a parent as a teacher in the same school and, until he gave up as we got older, we were required to be up betimes, have breakfast and board the old Ford Consul to head towards Townhead along the cobbled 'Expressway' towards Townhead. Very rarely were there advantages in having a parent at the school, as it occasionally meant a 'doing' from particular bullies. From time to time though, blind eyes were turned when it was known that I was a son of a colleague. That is, if the fact were known.

On one occasion I was found to be talking in class when I shouldn't have been, this by a formidable teacher called Major Toppin. 'You boy,' he shouted, 'have you been dragged up? What's your name?' There was a slight delay in his response when I told him, as well as a few sniggers from round about. The fact is that he was actually a very good chum of my father's and had been to a few football games with him. I wondered about that given his views of my father's parenting skills: 'Just sit down, boy, and keep quiet,' he said.

When I think about it there is probably enough here for a whole book on Glasgow Catholic education so I will only give you a couple of more stories in the meantime. Being a Catholic secondary school, we had many Italian and Polish derivatives: in fact, along with the Irish, the school was probably mostly populated with second-generation immigrants. And there was no such thing as racial discrimination; on the other hand, there was no such thing as political correctness. In fact, I once heard a Celtic supporter saying that he wasn't at all prejudiced as he hated all 'Blue-Noses' equally.

On one occasion, the famous Joe Barry, deputy heedy, came into my father's class in Parson Street. 'Mr Meighan', he said, 'I beg your pardon for interrupting [he was very formal], but do you have, in your class, a pupil by the name of "Smith"?' As it was my father's 'form' class, he knew right away that there was no such boy as 'Smith'. So Joe Barry left, only to return in two minutes to ask: 'Mr Meighan, would you please do me a great favour and check your register for the boy called "Smith".' Now my father was very used to playing Joe Barry's game, for remember that secondary schools in those days were run on military lines and the formalities and procedures were a game to teachers.

So from top to bottom, my father went through the class register to finally confirm that truly, there was no such 'Smith'. So again, Joe Barry hurried off, his black gown flowing behind him on his way through the door.

In three minutes he was back again. 'Mr Meighan, please forgive me again, but I have just realised my error. The fact is that the boy 'Smith' actually has some unpronounceable Polish name. I wonder if you have such a fellow here? Stand up, please, the boy with the long unpronounceable Polish name.'

At which my father called out to the hapless Polish lad, whose name I forget, 'stand up.'

'Ah,' said Joe Barry, 'The very fellow. Right "Smith", come with me!'

St Kentigern, Duke Street – part of 'The Mungo', my school. It has hardly changed since the 1960s.

Messages

It's peculiar but not unique to Glasgow. I once heard a radio interview with a bishop who had gone to Cambridge to study straight from Glasgow. When invited out by new friends, he apologised, saying that he had to go for the messages. 'What messages?' said the friends. 'Oh, just things that I need for the week.' 'What's in the messages?' 'I don't know yet. I'll see what they've got.' 'But who's giving you the messages?'… and so on.

He could have said that, 'when I get the messages, I'll take them home and put them in the press!'

Going for the messages was either a real hassle for me as a child or a treat depending on where I was sent. I don't suppose that I gave a moment's thought then that, as there were two younger brothers, it would be nice to help out.

In the fifties, we did not shop in the one place like we mostly do now. We were sent to the best and the cheapest shop for a particular thing. The balance between cheap and good meant that we sometimes had to go a long way to fill up the shopping bag: a stone of Kerr's Pinks in Elderslie Street, cakes at Ferguson's in Union Street, fish from Stockwell Street, 'Ashet pies' from Munro's the butchers.

The shops were wide and varied: the 'fruit shop' in Argyle Street where they boiled up fresh beetroot and provided toffee apples at Halloween; the Dublin Bakery was at Anderston Cross where the meaty smell of hot pies made your eyes water. I had to go sometimes to Coopers, who had a chain of shops, one at St Enoch Square. I don't know what I had to go there for, probably tea. Coopers was a shop where you could go to get freshly ground coffee. It was a smell and taste too sophisticated for the likes of me but the smell of ground coffee was brilliant when mixed in with the creamy smell of fresh butter and cheese, hams and spices.

There were bakers that you could go to in the night and get fresh, hot rolls that you could eat on their own or with a bit of butter and jam…

The smells of the shops were many and different but one brings back special memories. That was Brogan's butchers in Stobcross Street. The Misses Brogan were wonderful cheery spinsters, although I have no way of knowing how old they were. I remember them both wearing crisp starched blue dustcoats and the same kind of buns as Princess Leia wore in her hair in *Star Wars*.

'Cheap at half the price.'

The butcher's shop was high and large and you could see right in the back where it seemed that a number of blue and white-aproned butchers would be chopping and sawing. In the front the floor was covered in sawdust, and the smell of fresh-cut wood mingling with the smell of fresh raw meat was not unpleasant in that large airy shop. But the best thing about being sent there for a half-pound of steak mince or Lorne sausages was the fact that the Misses Brogan always had a sweetie for you and especially a Fry's Cream Bar.

While we are at it, I must tell you a story about a Hogmanay party that was held in a tenement in Argyle Street. In a narrow hallway off the 'stairheed', people sometimes kept cupboards or wardrobes. Following a few celebratory 'hawffs', one lugubrious and out-of-sorts Glaswegian came out of the 'hoose' and straight into an enormous wardrobe sitting in the hallway. He was heard to burst into tears and confess to some absent priest within the confessional wardrobe that he was sorry that he had 'knocked' money out of the Misses Brogan's cash drawer!

Incidentally, the Misses Brogan's was just a few doors away from Thomas Lipton's first grocery shop, opened by him in 1871 at the age of twenty-one. Sir Thomas Lipton was to become a millionaire and the founder of Lipton's Teas, still well-known today. The shop in Stobcross Street was to be the start of a tea empire which stretched throughout the world. The Liptons were Irish and had come to the Gorbals in Glasgow in 1850, like many others, as a result of the potato famine in Ireland. Lipton died in 1931 and is buried in the Southern Necropolis.

If you wanted stuff to kills flies or Esso Blue for your paraffin heater, or Aero glue or a million other things, you went to Gilfeathers at the corner of Anthony Street and Argyle Street. How he got so much stuff in there is anybody's guess but I do remember almost having to squeeze through one of the narrow doors, and I was thin!

'We belong to Glasgow': Marshall's of Glasgow.

Gilfeathers was where I was sent for Vim or Ajax or things like that. I remember getting refills for fly killers that must have been subject to some sort of chemical warfare regulation. You pumped the wet smelly death at the flies and watched them go down in squadrons. The shop smelt of wax polish, linseed oil, carbolic soap, Fairy soap, hessian rope and other wonderful dry-salter smells. Yes, a dry-salter was what Gilfeathers was because that's what it said above the door.

And while we are talking of the smell of vinegar, I have to tell you about a bit of an incident which could have stopped my fish suppering for all time. Directly across Argyle Street from us was Teacher's public house. I say public house as you got the impression that Teacher's felt themselves superior to the other pubs. Maybe this is because they were the only pub chain that was run by a distillery company: the others were mostly 'free houses' or run by the breweries.

Anyway, like many pubs Teacher's had an 'off-sales'. In this case and unusually, Teacher's sold their own brand of malt vinegar which you would buy from their 'off-sales', which was just a little room with a separate door but where you could look through a hatch and watch the men drinking in the polished mahogany bar-room.

I would be sent for the vinegar as needed over the road to Teacher's. One day I did so and as there was no one around on my return, for a reason that I can't remember, I took a sip and liked it. So I drank the lot and the ensuing illness was great aversion therapy, as was the 'shiriking' that I got on the return of the head of the family. Oh that this had worked so well in later life with lager, McEwan's and other sundry alcoholic beverages!

If you wandered into town you could go to the big department stores like Lewis's that had its own bank and we had a wee metal bankie shaped like a book and with a leather cover.

The problem was that it had a mechanism in so that you couldn't get a knife into it to get your money back out. You had to take it to Lewis's to be opened and then put your money in your account.

You could also go 'up the doonies' on the old wooden elevators before you were got by the scruff of the neck and ejected by the man in the blue uniform.

You could then go to Woolies – Woolworths to you – with its old squeaky wooden floors and its girls who traditionally disappeared to the end of the counter when you needed them. That's why they've made it self-service!

My father's the Lord Mayor of London
He cleans oot the middens at night
And when he comes home in the morning
His shoes are all covered in sh....
Shine up your buttons with Brasso
Only tuppence a tin
You can get it in Woolies for nothing
As long as there's naebody in.
(Sung to the tune of 'My Bonnie Lies over the Ocean')

In case I forget, there was also the smell of the message bag, this being normally of musty potatoes. The message bag, kept in the press, was essential to daily shopping and was normally a leather or canvas carrier with straps at either side about the size of a modern-day plastic bag but less deep. Every woman carried one at all times in case bargains were to be had.

I don't remember it being sissy. It was just something you used. In case you don't know, we didn't have plastic carrier bags back then and there was no argument about 'do you want a bag?' We always carried 'a bag for life'. You would go into the fruit shop to get a half-stone of Kerr's Pinks or Ayrshires. These would be weighed in the scales with the big brass weights. You would then hold the bag open and the totties would be poured into the bag in a cloud of dust.

Then you could wander down the street, seeing how fast you could swing the bag round and round over your head. Inevitably you would hit some poor passer-by or a handle would break and the bag and totties would fly everywhere.

While we are about it, there was hardly any plastic, never mind baggies. While we had Bakelite, plastics were only gradually introduced. I think I remember the first plastic basin which was made of what was spelled polyethylene but I thought was pronounced 'polythighlene'!

Deliveries

Of course, you could have your messages delivered as most things could be in those days. Those were the days of butcher boys' bikes, of which there was always at least one outside Magee's poultry shop, the poultry shop which had a hut behind it where you could go and see the chickens being poked through a funnel and having their necks twisted by hand, then their heads and legs cut off. We used to gather up the legs and throw them at girls.

Anyway, deliveries. It was the thing to get a job delivering things. As for me I think I stuck a week as a milk boy for the Garden Rose Dairy in Argyle Street. Well excuse me, but frankly the effort of climbing tenement stairs lugging bottles of milk before breakfast nearly killed me! Actually when I think of it, it wasn't the milk bottles, it was lugging the crates in a huge metal trolley almost to the Kelvingrove Park that did it. I didn't think I was that much of a weakling… oh, all right then, I suppose I was. Anyway, the chap who owned the Garden Rose was nice enough to pay me for the week. So besides a short-lived foray into selling sticks from a bogie (see bogies) that was it until I inherited a delivery round from my brother Martin. I can't remember how he actually got it but it was a real 'skoosh' and very sedate. It was for the Castlebank Laundry at Argyle Street opposite Elderslie Street. His job was to deliver dry cleaning and laundry to the clients of that establishment. Now the work was not difficult as the laundry was well wrapped up in nice brown paper with string and he used an old pram (in which Stephen used to be pushed) to deliver the goods.

What I hadn't known or thought about as I took it over for reasons that I can't remember, was that, of course, those who can afford to pay for dry cleaning to be delivered are wont to be generous in general and in fact the tips were rather good. And it was at times to suit, namely just after school rather than some unfriendly hour of the dawn. I could have had a career there.

The Dear Green Place

As I think about it I can taste the American cream soda, and the sweet Italian vanilla ice cream. Kelvingrove Park was the best park: there were other parks, but Kelvingrove was our nearest and where we headed of a weekend or of an evening.

We lived near the park, at the bottom of North Street. We would set off in a pack, carrying our preferred bottles of American cream soda, Irn-Bru or lemonade, all of these being 'ginger'. All the way up North Street we would jostle, jump and take a slug of ginger, have a burping competition, exploding and with noses streaming, continue. Past the 'brokies', the remains of bombed-out buildings, now cleared. Over St Vincent Street, past Charing Cross station and then

From the top of Kelvingrove Park.

to start our ascent past the posh houses up Park Terrace, still with their stone mounting blocks for getting into carriages or onto your horse.

Here you could have a choice – to start at the bottom of the park or go up Park Circus to the top. My favourite was starting at the bottom gate because there you could get an ice-cream cone from the 'Tally Man' with the wee three-wheeled ice-cream cart; the sweet smell of vanilla ice cream in a cone or luxuriously in a 'slider' or decadently as a '99' with chocolate vermicelli or raspberry sauce. Smell the sweetness and taste the combination of the cold ice cream, chocolate and sauce. 'Ye cannae whack it!'

He would be at the gate on a hot day in summer. Take the ice cream and you have to be quick as it melts in the heat. Start to wander up the main path, yards of flowers on either side. Though you don't know much about flowers, the smell seems to be intensified by the heat. Inevitably, there are bees floating by and everywhere the shouts of children, the wailings of babies and the chatter of people.

In the fountain – where you are not supposed to be – splashing up and down. Sliding on the big shute in the swing park, hiding in the bushes and getting whistled at by the 'parkie'.

Why the photograph here of the statue of Lord Roberts? Because I go there when I can. It's at the highest point on the park from where you can see Gilmorehill, the University of Glasgow. You can see the Museum and Art Gallery as well as a large expanse of Glasgow south of the river. It is my favourite spot in all of Glasgow even now.

Must have been a lean-to!

Many years ago, in the fifties, as an altar boy at St Patrick's parish in Anderston, I would be sent to assist a senior Glasgow Catholic priest – a Monsignor with Mass at his residence, 'The Vicariat' in Park Circus. At six in the morning, I would take my bike from the rooftop washhouse and carry it down the stairs. I would set off up North Street, my legs pumping to get momentum to carry me as far up the hill as possible. Then over St Vincent Street, again speeding up before having to push up the hill towards Park Circus; here at 6.30 a.m. on a cool spring morning, Glasgow was coming to life. You may think of Glasgow as a black diamond in the 1960s, but at that time on a morning, before the fires were lit, the air was clean and clear. The birds sang and the windows and roofs way across the river glittered. The smell from flowers and trees rising from the park would fill my nostrils. My cheeks would be red with effort and my chest heaving. So I would lean on the granite parapet and just quietly smell the morning coming to life and listen to the faraway early traffic of the Dear Green Place. There, you were at the top of the world and you could do anything. 'I'm the king of the castle and you're a dirty wee rascal.'

The Molendinar

On the other hand, I was very disappointed recently when I revisited my old school, St Kentigern's, which was part of St Mungo's Academy was when I was there. The school is now a business centre and that is very good. However, between the school playground and the old and sad Great Eastern Hotel (but not really a hotel) is, I think, the only remaining uncovered part of the famous Molendinar Burn which has featured in so many stories and memories of Glasgow.

In fact, one outing we would do as a family was to retrace the Molendinar from the Clyde away back up to Hogganfield Loch where it has its source. At school, it was a ploy to climb over the railings and try to go up the tunnel out of which came the Molendinar to run about 100 yards before disappearing under the High Street goods yard. I can tell you it was pretty smelly then, although we didn't seem to notice.

The Molendinar.

THE LADY WELL

RESTORED 1836 ∻ REBUILT 1874
BY THE
MERCHANTS HOUSE OF GLASGOW

The Lady Well.

On revisiting the burn I was appalled at the state of it because although in the photograph it looks like an idyllic little burn it is in fact an open sewer. Surely this doesn't still flow directly into the Clyde? 'Somebody should do something.'

While we are in the area, I might as well tell you of my surprise and delight to find that the Lady Well is still in existence. This well, used since the time of St Mungo, fell into disuse in the 1800s, probably because it is set into the wall of the Necropolis where there are a lot of bodies buried. We passed this well on our way up to our school canteen (we called it 'the dinner school' for some reason). The roads are now re-aligned and it can be found in an obscure cul-de-sac behind the Tennent Caledonian Wellpark Brewery. Go and see it. It's a historic site.

The Close

'Ooooopen!' we would shout at the foot of the stair to let our mum know we were home. Unfortunately, we sometimes forgot about Doctor MacGuire's surgery on the first floor. Before the surgery opened there would be a queue of people waiting up the stairway almost to our door on the second floor. Having shouted 'oooopen!' once or twice we then would have to endure the embarrassment of the sniggers or stares of the people in the queue.

Argyle Street.

My brother Jim reminded me of the day I got my own back. I was heading up the stairs, ready to go past the long queue which I thought was longer than usual. Just for the hell of it, I tried the door in passing and, lo and behold, it was open. Apparently, Doctor MacGuire told my mother later, the people in the queue were a bit miffed at being shown up by a wee boy. Nobody loves a smartarse!

We lived up a close in Anderston. But it was no ordinary close like a close in a back street where nothing happened: it was a very exiting close all told. Of course, every close has its ups and downs! The fact that it was right beside a pub and opposite two others inclined it to smell like a public toilet at certain times with a low odour at other times. There was the smell of town gas too. While I think that our close was converted to electric lights I very clearly remember the lamp-lighter going up the stairs with a pole, reaching up and turning on the gas before lighting it with his paraffin lamp at the end of the stick. The gas would go on with a blue 'pop', the mantle would warm up and the lamp would settle down to a white hissing light.

Oor Close

Atween a barber's pole and store, near where they hulkin' tramcars roar, oor close extends in tunnelled strength, its funnelled, soond-collecting length.

Some Summer days the close mooth swells, wi' thrawin' bairnies deefenin' yells, as twixt the backcourt and the street, they clatter through on fleein' feet.

On Winter days when school is 'in', the heid is free frae echoed din, an' gars a bedded, ailin' wight tae weary for the noisesome night.

There's ither days the year a' roond, oor ears are dingin' wi' the soond o' clackin' hoosewives rantin' fair, aboot their neebours on the stair.

On ither nights o' sun or sleet, when lad and lass taegither meet, each hidden corner amplifies, the courtin' couples' fervent sighs.

There's ne'er a blade o' grass tae see, and grimy sparra's ken nae tree, the backclose refuge only leads tae washin'-hoose and midden heid.

Yet, frae whit airt the wind may blaw, wi' sunshine, rain or hail, or snaw, frae a' the elements tae cower, 'Oor Close' provides the sheltered bower.

Andrew Chalmers Lillie

While Glasgow still had many a sign which said 'No Loitering', our close was a favourite place for looking out on the world. Many a time had my dad or Tommy Ballantine stood there looking at the passing world before going off 'to see a man about a dog.' Actually it was years later I realised he was going off to the pub. Either that or he saw a lot of men about a lot of dogs that I never saw, then ended up in the pub anyway.

And our building (I refuse to call it a tenement out of pure snobbery) looked on to a back close. No matter that this area contained a large garage and warehouse and a yard in which lorries and old horse-drawn wagons were stored, it was a great place for playing cowboys and Indians and best falls.

It has been pointed out to me that I should explain what 'best falls' is. Best falls was normally played with chums immediately after emerging from the cinema having experienced at first hand how the cowboys or soldiers did it. You would play cops and robbers, cowboys and so on. We shot at one another with imaginary Tommy guns, with all the requisite pretend noises: 'rat-tat-tat, bang, bang. Oh you got me…' Whereupon you would be hit by an imaginary bullet and take a dive and points (sort of) would be awarded for the best fall. When I think about it, it's actually very like what modern footballers do when slightly molested now!

The garage was where my father worked. This was in his Brylcreem and motor-oil days before he moved on to smell of Brylcreem, science lab and school. That yard was always full of activity and I was even allowed into the garage until the day I drilled my finger. I still have the finger but I was not encouraged thereafter to enter the garage.

Argyle Street
now.

Anyway, furniture vans came and went through the pend into Argyle Street. At the weekend and even sometimes during the holidays, we dodged the lorries to play rounders in the court because it was about the biggest back court that we knew. One time I was (supposed to be) looking after my youngest brother Stephen, who then decided to head in a straight line right through the pend into Argyle Street.

Strange, the complete memories you have. I do not remember the first two cars that hit him but I remember him sitting there in his little reins on the cobbles with his legs underneath a red MG Midget, unscathed. I can still remember the petrified face of the guy in the Midget as I gathered up Stephen and a crowd surrounded us. He was unscathed and of an age that he survived fine till we began to realise that he must have actually been banged on the head, or maybe that's just him.

Back to the pend, and even at night there was activity. Long-distance drivers would come back from England or the north of Scotland with their loads. The foreman lived in the block next to ours and in the night you would hear a lorry roar through the pend, the door open and then a shout, 'Wulfie.' I am sure his name was Alfie, but it sounded like Wulfie. The window banged up and you heard the rattle of keys on the cobbles as they were flung through the window.

Then the big sliding door being unlocked and slid back, the lorry moving into the garage and the door being closed: the driver would then take the keys up the stair to go through Alfie's door and his footsteps would recede through the pend into the night – and in those days it was into the night and into silence because Argyle Street and the city were quiet except for the occasional faraway blast of a ship's horn or the rattle of a maintenance car on the tramlines.

Occasionally we got itinerants who would come into the centre of the back court and sing such dreadful songs that I swear that those who opened their windows to throw out pennies did it to get rid of them. But, you know, there was never a bad word for them.

Going into our long close between the Queen's Arms and Davy Ireland's Newspapers, you passed the pipe where we broke penny dainties. Penny dainties were large McCowan's toffees that you would put into your mouth all at the same time if you really wanted to choke or mangle your teeth irredeemably. I fear I still suffer from that malady myself.

'The Stairheed'.

No. You had to break them in two, and everyone had a special place to break them because it needed a special touch otherwise they would not break cleanly in two but shatter into pieces. My place was a bracket on a pipe at the foot of our stairs. I shared it with others, of course. Such was the community in the close!

Doctor MacGuire's surgery was on the first floor, as was a manufacturer of something or other, spectacles maybe. It was peculiar to find workshops up closes but sometimes you did.

We shared our landing, or 'stairheed', with Mrs Gray and Mrs Macadam; above us were the Ballantines, the Thompsons and old Mrs Boyle, whose ashes (coal fire, not personal) I used to take to the midden.

Talking of coal fires and ashes, of course, the coal had to first of all get to the house. This was by way of the coalman, originally on a horse and cart. As he passed we would shout out the number of bags or, in many instances he would simply come up the close, expecting to sell coal. With his mangled black leather waistcoat and cap, he held a hundredweight of coal in a black sack over his back and would do this all day long.

As he came into the close he would shout 'Co-ell!' We would come to the door and tell him how many bags were needed. He would come up and down the stairs till the bunkers of all those

My mother wearing my school bag.

in the close who needed coal were filled. While some people did have their coal in varnished bunkers in the kitchen (really), we did not as we had a wee cupboard between the hall and the bathroom. Oooh yes! We were quite posh in having a bathroom. The coalman would come in, banging the bag on the door, squeezing into the bunker area and hefting the coal bag off his shoulders into the bunker with a loud 'thunk'. Then he would pull the bottom of the sack and out would come the coal rumbling into the bunker in a cloud of black, dry-smelling dust.

As far as I remember, the coal came in fairly large chunks and we would have to break it up using my mother's old fire axe. (She had been a firewoman – and here she is above wearing a gas-mask bag during the war. We used these as school bags for ages and they were really cool, that is until tartan duffel bags came along!). We also could get coal briquettes and these smelled slightly differently from coal. These were bricks of coal dross which burned more slowly and maybe were cheaper, I don't remember.

But wonder of wonders, our secret was that we had a flat roof and a boiler house on the roof. The roof was a square terrace surrounded by a stone balustrade. We didn't know then how desirable that would be now. The downside was, of course, that it was perpetually covered in a layer of black soot as it was surrounded by chimneys. But you could easily climb from our

Above: Towards the university.

Opposite left: Grannie's stairheed cludgie.

Opposite right: In front of the fire.

flat roof up to the next pitched roof where someone there kept doos (pigeons) in a dookit (pigeon loft). My cousin Angela, who lived in Macintyre Street, reminded me of the time that I was calmly and quietly reading *The Beano* on the aforementioned pinnacle when I was reported to the police who, in the guise of a very large body having climbed five storeys, appeared as a puffing head over the wall that separated the pitched roof from the flat roof. I could hardly make out the strangulated plea: 'would... you... come... down... out... of... there... for ★ ★ ★ sake!'

You could see over most of the other tenements to the cranes on the river Clyde or up to the university and churches in Park Circus. On a hot sunny day you could sit and bake and smell the roof tar melting and hear the passing trams and traffic far below. I was 'Up on the Roof' long before The Drifters. Above is one of our views.

You inevitably got to know many of the closes in your area, many of them fairly smelly things. It was quite unusual then for cats to be neutered and so the smell of cat was common. Cats, as far as I remember, were more common than dogs. I suppose Glaswegians then had the good sense not to keep dogs in a tenement. There were closes with wally tiles, that is tiles that were glazed. The further you got towards the park and posher houses, the wallier the tiles would become. These days the tiles off the walls are very collectable, but the good news is that it's not very easy to get them off without breaking them.

Some of the closes also had pretty windows with red and blue borders. But some closes were the bee's knees: women regularly took their turns to whitewash the borders in closes as well as polish the kerbs with Cardinal Red. You always knew a well-kept close by the fresh smell of polish and the chalky smell of whitewash.

Murder, murder polis,
Three stairs up
The wuman in the middle door
Hit me wae a cup'
Ma heeds aw broken ma face is aw cut
Murder, murder polis,
Three stairs up

No last night but the night before
Three wee monkeys came tae ma door
One wi a trumpet and one wi a drum
And one wi a pancake stuck tae its bum!

And, incidentally, it was Glaswegians that invented 'yuppies', for every morning you could hear the shrill cry through every close in Glasgow: 'Y'up?' 'Aye, am up.'

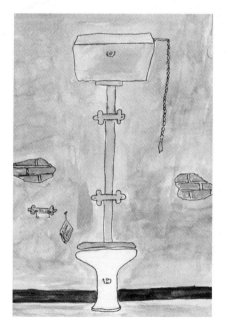 

Kitchen Life

I can still feel the smooth edge of the tiled surround and the rough edge where the poker sat. I can still run my Dinky toy along the surround for it to fall off the edge on to the mat. I can still see my little brother and me playing with the Dinky toys on the mat in front of the fire or building a house from a construction kit.

I can still smell the smoke and feel the heat from the fire, the big chunks of coal sizzling and popping, the burst of blue gas hissing and dying; the kitchen clock ticking and my father in his armchair studying. I can still look around and see the small dimensions of our kitchen, the cooker in one corner, the box bed in another, the kitchen sideboard and door, the television in its old brown case like an intruder. 'It'll never take on, you know.'

Above left: Colonial emigrant Leslie Ballantine in our kitchen.

Above right: From our roof towards Central Station.

While there was also a bedroom, these were the confines of our lives where we lived out our hopes and aspirations for the future. In the 1950s we didn't have a clue. You lived in a room and kitchen and what we knew was that the only way out was through education. 'You stick in son… if ah hud your chances' – time and again we would hear it.

My father took the chance of becoming a teacher through the Government's Special Recruitment Scheme. This meant that he went to 'uni' when we were young and would study at nights while mammie would work, mostly in Wypers bar, to support us. Tough times, but in the fifties most people had it that way and did not complain. Then they mostly took measures to move on.

Many people lived in 'single ends', which was just a room and kitchen. Theoretically, ours was not a single end as it, unusually, had a full bathroom. Our tenement was substantially built by the Weavers' Society of Anderston, and had it not been right in the way of the new Kingston Bridge it may well have been preserved.

Anyway, six of us – my parents and three brothers – lived in these two rooms. Don't ask me because it's hard to explain, but we all fitted in and many families had more children than us. In fact, one of my earliest memories was of swapping houses with the Ballantines as they had a bigger family than us. Leslie Ballantine was a good pal of mine and, after some initial forays, followed his sisters to America to stay. We lost touch, but here he is in our kitchen.

Virtually every family had relatives in the colonies. Ours were mostly in New York, and only infrequently did we get to see them. I do know that, in common with many others in Great Britain, they would send us parcels of stuff during the war. I can't remember any foodstuffs but I do remember getting books, particularly the *Illustrated Classics*, which I loved.

You know, I don't remember general smells other than that of the fire or cooking fish and chips on Friday, or bacon on a Sunday. But I do remember the particular smells of my mother's hand cream, my father's Brylcreem, and the smell of fly spray or of a newly opened packet of bread.

We ate in the kitchen and my parents slept in the box bed unless my mother had to be in a bed with a baby: then I got to share the kitchen bed with my dad. The sounds of Glasgow were different on that side of the building and I would listen for ages to the faraway city.

There was the incident of the blue tea. I used to get blamed for everything including, I might add, sawing drawers off an old sewing-machine stand. As if I would. Get away with you see!

Anyway I may as well take the blame for the blue tea. The kettle being boiled, the tea was 'masked', and then poured out into cups. 'That's a funny colour,' said dad. More tea was poured and the consensus was that the tea was indeed an outrageous, almost Glasgow Rangers, blue-nose shade of tea!

The teapot, being looked into by one and all, threw no light on the mystery: the kettle now being focused on required a long spoon to go delving in and to fish out – a blue sock! I can't remember if one of us had to go to school with different-shaded socks.

When we weren't playing with Dinky toys we played with what we could get our hands on. Upturned kitchen tables used as boats were a favourite. My mother came into the kitchen one day to find me aged five or six, sitting two storeys up on the window ledge at the sink, filling milk bottles with water and emptying them into the back court below:

I'm a little teapot
Short and stout
Here's my handle, here's my spout
When the kettle boils
Hear me shout
Tip me up and pour me out

(With actions, by the way.)

Street Life

First of all, given their importance, I have to have a brief word about stanks. For those unfamiliar with the term, in Glasgow a 'stank' is a street drain of any sort. Obviously, stanks must figure prominently in any book on smells; on the other hand, it is amazing how young boys can ignore smells while they are having fun.

Stanks can be smelly things, but my memory is of them being particularly useful in winter for playing with the snowy sludge and making dams. We were forced to wear galoshes by my parents. For those of you who may not know, galoshes were rubber covers for shoes and were very practical in the snow and rain, if embarrassing. At that time, most shoes were made of leather and prone to leaking. I wonder whether if they were popular today you could get Nike galoshes. That would be something.

At any other time of the year, stanks were most useful for playing stankie. It depended very much on the shape of the stank, and one in front of the station at Anderston Cross was a favourite.

Stankie is a game played with jorries (marbles) on a stank – the stank has to be symmetrical, made of regular round holes capable of holding the jorries. The game itself was about attempting to get your jorrie in the round hole next to your opponent on your turn so that you could keep his jorrie. (Girls didn't play stankie.) The stank pictured here would be perfect if you were to clean out the holes with the thing on your big penknife that was used for taking stones out of horses' hooves.

I can see us there playing with our jorries on the hot summer pavement, playing stankie and then moving on to something else, maybe five stones, or investigating the stables or the closes before deciding that we had enough for a shared bag of chips from Dannie's before tea.

'Stankie'.

And in passing, I remember the big stanks in front of buildings. You can still see these occasionally. They were made of cast iron and were about 4ft long by 2ft wide; some had square holes filled with thick glass and some had open slats. They were for allowing light into basements. The open ones and those with broken glass would fill up with smelly rubbish. Occasionally someone would drop money down them. A ploy was to take a stick, go to Mackintosh's garage and get a dod of thick motor grease on it. The money would generally stick to the grease and you would be able to get another poke of chips. Or you might get rewarded for retrieving someone's key, although they were a bit heavier in those days, before the Yale key. A 'check' key, we called it.

While we are talking about penknives, I have just remembered that this was only one of the things that you carried about in your pockets, which never seemed big enough. Of course, the contents varied according to the time of the year. My friends and I would at times carry a tin pea-shooter and a pocketful of hard green peas for firing at one another. This was a milder form of eye attack than the bow and arrow but could still cause some damage. And with the small pea-shooter you could easily hide it and act daft:

'It wisnae me mister, a big boy did it n' ran awae.'
'Ah'll batter your melt in if ah catch ye.'

There was also the magnifying glass in the summer for burning holes in paper, hands or people's trousers. You could also carry a piece of brown sticking tape. This you would wet and, making a crease in your skin, put it over the crease till it stuck. Then you would take the paper away slowly and you would have a brilliant scar on which you could put red ink and pretend that you had been sliced open!

You always carried Dubble-Bubble bubble gum; either unused or half-chewed as you never knew when it would come in handy. There might be matchboxes or books for your collection, picked up from the street; cap guns or potato guns or a plethora of thingies that were given away in comics with names such as whizzers, a disc that, when you pulled a string in each hand, whizzed round making a hissing sound. You might have a whistle for annoying purposes, a catapult, bubble-gum cards for playing a game in which you threw the cards against the wall and the person who'd thrown the nearest got to keep them. I was quite good at it.

The day I got knocked down was memorable in as much as it was by about the only American car in Glasgow at that time. It belonged to the owner of the Italian ice-cream shop on Argyle Street.

Above left and right: These two stanks are no good for 'stankie'.

Right: Perfect for stankie!

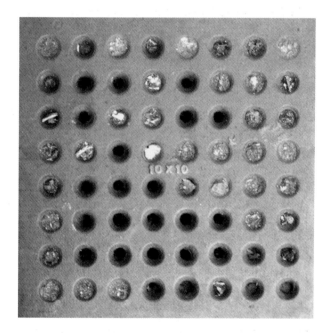

I was being chased over the street by Danny Fish, wielding a stick with a nail in it. What I was doing to merit this I don't know except maybe straying on to his territory in the high back close across the street. Anyway, here I was haring across the street to be mown down by a Chevy. I do remember the confusion and several people either trying to pick me up or hold me down till an ambulance came. I remember the white ambulance arriving, but the last thing I was going to do was get in. In the same way that I was thrown out of nursery school, they finally relented at my unhelpful attitude and I again sloped off, more cautiously and a bit more slowly to my stair.

As for Danny Fish, I don't remember seeing him again after that. I wonder if it cured him of chasing people with sticks with nails in them. It certainly made me a wee bit cautious in crossing roads, which is possibly a good thing. It wasn't very long after that in returning home down North Street from some ploy, I could see an enormous crowd of people. Getting nearer, I could

Section of stank
with greenery.

see that they were gathered round a double-decker bus stopped in exactly the same spot where I had been run over by the Chevy, between our corner and The Gaiety Bar across the street.

I spotted my father at the back of the crowd and said 'Hi daddy, what's happening?' He turned such a pale face on me that I thought that he was ill. All he said was, 'where were you?' and 'get up that stair!'

Of course I sneaked out very soon after to find that the bus had run down a child of my age whose body was under a sack. His head was about 10ft away under another sack. The bus driver was being comforted in the bus. I was awestruck by this and by the size and silence of the enormous crowd, that over a period of time began to drift away. I don't know if it made me any the less adventurous but I suspect that seeing my father's face also slowed me down a bit.

Talking of public transport, there was always the bogie beloved by many a Glasgow boy. The bogie had a standard shape and size. It was made out of available planks, the chassis being about 3ft long and about 1ft wide. At one end there was a wooden box with one of the sides removed. The box was placed sideways at the end of the plank so that your bum could settle back into the box. You then had two pram wheels under the box and at the far end you put a wooden axle under the plank with a nail or bolt to enable it to swivel.

At either end of the axle you put two large wheel bearings if you could get them, or two small pram wheels. Attached to either end of the axle was a cord which you used to guide the bogie as well as your feet (which rested against the axle), and in this way your heels could be used as a brake. Some posh varieties also had a stick attached to the side of the box that could be used as a brake on the wheels.

The only thing you then needed was a hill. Now one of the most dangerous times of the year for the pedestrian Glaswegian was the first week of the school holidays in which bogies miraculously appeared at the top of steep pavements to sweep all and sundry before them.

Oh, and they were of particularly welcome use for Guy Fawkes Night when most of us celebrated the demise through immolation of that very well-known Catholic gentleman. I always wondered why good Catholics like us were allowed to do so. Anyway, what we would do is to

A Glasgow bogie.

build a Guy, which was really a dressed-up dummy of the bold Mr Fawkes (I used to think it was Guy Fox). This we would then parade through the streets on our bogies, holding out cups for donations to the fighting fund which allowed us to buy squibs and other fireworks to celebrate that good day by blowing up milk bottles and old ladies' letter boxes. All good clean fun.

In the meantime, sundry others would be gathering up old doors, lino and carpets in order to build their local bonfires. They had to set guards as other gangs would be trying to steal our fuel so that they would have the biggest bonfire. It wasn't unusual to have spent many days building up a major fuel dump only to get there and find it had been well and truly knocked (stolen). Bastards!

Now, if young people still spend a good part of their outdoor time in pursuit of bearings or pram wheels I would give some advice – never get involved in consortium approaches to bogie building. In the first place, you never know who owns the bogie and the recriminations that take place over such machines can lead to bitter acrimony for years.

I say this from experience, as once I got involved in joint ownership of a bogie with one William Rooney who resided above The Gaiety Cinema in Argyle Street. Now, we had started the gathering process and had got so far as to acquire a set of pram wheels before the trouble started: the said bold William had laid claim to the wheels, which, in time, no doubt, would mean that further claims on the future bogie were sure to come. Well, one thing led to another and heads were lost. Well, with what I thought was the justice of Solomon, I broke the chassis wheels in two and handed him one end with his wheel. Summoning my dignity I walked away with my single wheel attached. And here is my message to Mr Rooney: I still have it. It's mine and no yours!

Our playgrounds were the streets and the brokies and they had their own purposes. There were brokies or streets particular to football and there was a very special brokie in Cadogan Street which was a Mecca for those with bikes because, long before there were BMX tracks, we had a brilliant four-acre brokie that was a real treat for dirt-bike racing. That's where we headed the first week in the summer holidays when the word would go round that there was a race.

High backs, Springburn by Andrew Chalmers Lillie.

The flat roof (high back court) behind Alex Mair's building in Bishop Street was brilliant for tennis at Wimbledon time. There would be dozens of young people looking for fun in the summer and we knew where to find it. One of the best places to play was where they were building the new St Patrick's Primary School in North Street. Now we were used to buildings being demolished and using them as brokies: no one was yet used to building sites, and strangely enough the security was minimal.

So dozens of kids pounced on the site in the evening to use the sand like a beach and make huts out of the timber. I don't know how long this went on for but one day while we were playing, a shout went up: 'Police'. Kids went everywhere, through McGee's Pend, up North Street, along School Wynd or up to William Street. I headed round the south of the Scotland Electricity Board transformer building, only to be grabbed by the wrist by an enormous policeman. Bearing in mind that this was my very first confrontation with a policeman and I was only about ten, how was I to know that you weren't to assault them? Anyway, I amazed myself by giving this bobby a right kick on the shin. I was probably equally amazed that he let me go and I swiftly made it round the corner, across the street, up the close and into my house to peek round the corner up North Street to watch for the bobby.

It simply didn't cross my mind that the bobby was probably too embarrassed to even say that he had been kicked by a wean. On the other hand, I am beginning to panic that, what with the new developments in DNA testing, he may still be able to come after me if he still has the bit of skin from my arm that I must have left with him.

My mother 'clyping' me to 'the polis'.

Me looking out for 'the polis'.

Fags

Smoking was a part of street life in as much as it could not be done at home by me. Although my father smoked Senior Service before he gave them up I can never remember him smoking at home either. Perhaps that's because smoking was such a way of life then, and you probably did not notice the fug caused by it.

I first smoked when I was about thirteen, I suppose, probably out of sheer bravado: round the corner of some dyke with pals and a packet of five Bristols. I think the alternative was five Woodbines but we thought Bristols were a bit more up-market.

There was no way, of course, of smoking at school because the very idea of being caught by Brother John or Mr Seenan was just not on: also, the idea of being caught by my father was another reason for not doing it. And I wonder if he actually noticed.

Besides, I probably hardly ever smoked but the fags' use would gradually creep up on you and you would get addicted and I suppose that's the way it works. I don't smoke now but it was an effort not to do so.

I always wondered why those people who smoked had such a downer on those of us who aspired to be smokers. They were trying to teach us other things but did not want us to do what they did? Get real!

Like becoming blood brothers, it was probably more the bravado, the secrecy and the ritual that we did it for and to be like the big boys! And it did have a ritual. If a packet of five was not few enough you could buy 'tipped singles' from the wee shops. And I'm sure that the Medical Officers of Health must also have been appalled at the sharing of cigarettes: it was very common for pals to buy a tipped single and then smoke it in 'limits' which was three puffs each. If it wasn't a tipped cigarette and you made a wet mess of the end you were readily accused of making a 'coo's arse' of it, and this was not a very manly thing to be accused of. Of course, if you were able to blow smoke rings, that gave you extra big-boy points.

Now collecting cigarette cards was before my time as they seemed to have stopped doing that while moving on to enclosing coupons so that you could buy things from a catalogue. 'Embassy' and 'Kensitas' coupons became a commodity and you could see adverts for '1,000 Embassy' coupons in shop windows.

What I did used to do – I was shown this by my father – was to make the cigarette packets into little tanks with turrets made out of the silver paper. You could have little wars with your tanks. Alternatively you could turn the silver paper into little Scottish cups and line these up to shoot with your pea-shooter. My father was a dab hand at sticking these to the roof and to this day I don't know how he did it as he never told me. It reminds me that in Woodside Road or St George's Road there was a shop with a little Scottie Dog about a foot high made out of Capstan packets.

Now, I have a book which I recently managed to find again as I remember having it when I was very young. It is called *Glasgow Our City*. It was published in 1957 when I was seven and it is hilarious and I recommend it to you. The funniest aspect of it is the characters who appear to 'talk with jorries in their mooths' but also to use phrases like 'By Jove'. In Partick?

Unbelievably and totally true, in the last chapter of the book the characters debate what Glasgow will be like in 2007: 'I might even recognise some of the bailies or tobacco lords as I hurriedly get out of their way!' Maybe that's because they can't now smoke in the pubs and are standing in the doorways?

As one Glasgow policeman said to the other: 'Lend us a fag till the shops shut.' And there is a good chance of them asking, 'can I have one for Ron?' 'Ron who?' 'Later on!' 'Have you got a light, Mac?' 'No, but I've got a heavy overcoat!'

Glasgow Police Labs checking my DNA!

Dublin Christy, 1960

Dublin Christy slouched along the pavement in 1960 in his thick black herring-bone coat, open and flapping, his squat Irish body lurching from side-to-side in the gait of the drunk; his felt hat greasy and battered, his brogues open to the wind and flapping. We had an expression for the Glasgow drunk's progress: 'three steps forward and two backwards.' How slow would be his progression from pub to sweet shop?

And always at his feet his mongrel dog, dappled brown and white, a ferrety, ratty kind of yappy thing. Never on a lead. Going on ahead, scouting behind, jumping up and down on everyone, sometimes suffering the inglorious belt of a boot and then skulking, till it forgot the fear and pain and started over again.

I remember Dublin Christy for a very particular reason and for more general reasons: for the particular reason that Dublin Christy's dog bit me. The shock sends me back to the exact place, outside Lloyd's Bar beside The Gaiety Picture House on Argyle Street, in Anderston. It caused me to have my first experience of a tetanus injection in the backside. This took me by surprise but there was no end to me getting cut, scraped or standing on nails. Visits to 'Yorkhill' Children's Hospital were very regular, particularly in the summer. What concerned me most was the thought of the dreaded 'lockjaw'. Along the same lines as 'forkytails' climbing into your ears, we were regaled with stories of the football player who got a cut and whose jaw seized up and he died on the pitch.

As well as that there was the fear of rabies. I am quite sure that Dublin Christy's dog was nowhere near rabid but the effect took hold. Almost as much as the fear of choking to death like the girl whose statue was in the cemetery in North Street. Little sympathetic bastards our friends were then, as well as being knowledgeable about horrible ways to die.

But I remember Dublin Christy for another more general reason: Dublin was the epitome of the homecoming hero now unwanted. I don't know if that specifically applied to him but I remember his ilk: the city centre had many of what my old headmaster called the 'Pas Perdus', the lost feet. Many of these had suffered and lost in the war and could find no respite. I can see them wandering around Anderston, sitting at Anderston Cross, retuning to their 'Model' lodging houses in Pitt Street, Cheapside Street, Clyde Street and many other lodging houses throughout the city.

I was born in the Rottenrow Maternity Hospital on 27 March 1950 becoming at once a 'baby boomer', that class of babies born at a time when the horizons were clear once again and life was getting back to a form of normality for those affected by their great war. We were not then troubled by a Cuba Crisis and the beginning of the Cold War; the great spy novels had also yet to be written.

For it was only five years before I was born that the Second World War had ended, yet the signs were there. The signs of war wounds on fathers' bodies, the signs that they would not talk about; the signs of war on troubled minds, signs that they could not talk about. And everywhere, the signs of bombing. Whole blocks flattened and empty as they would be for a good twenty years to come. Single spaces in tenement streets testifying to a single bomb destroying families and friends.

The back courts held brick air-raid shelters roofed with concrete. These would be bricked up or turned into stores and were to become our 'dykes' for leaping to and from. Many city buildings were still coated with green and brown camouflage paint and they were still digging up unexploded bombs. Men were still wearing their 'demob' suits and many things like sugar were still rationed.

The 1950s were a rootless time and men and women drifted here and there. Some took their own lives, unable to cope with the demands of society. That same 1950s society was very concerned with health and welfare but unable to cope with difficult minds.

But we move on and remember the Dublin Christies or the man who sat every day in front of a hoarding at Glasgow Cross, his head constantly shaking from side to side. I asked my father about him as we walked to the Barras: 'poor man', he said, 'he got shell shock in the war.' I wonder if we have moved on?

Wee chooky birdie, to lo lo
Laid an egg on the windae so
The windae so began to crack
Wee chooky birdie
Quack, quack, quack.

The Chimney Fire

The chimney fire was a scourge in Glasgow in the 1950s and '60s although there were those who always said that it would save you the cost of having the chimney swept. The first hint of a chimney fire amongst the tenements would be the acrid sulphurous smell. It's strange that nothing else smells like a chimney on fire in my memory. It is an acrid concentrated sooty business which claws its way down your nostrils and into your lungs. It is almost solid, burning carbon rather than burning coal.

Then you look around to see where the fire is and there it is, away above the roofs. The lum like a steam engine in full power belching black, black smoke; the windows crash up and all over the heads come out and stare. The children in the street gawp, scream and point.

Argyle Street.

And inside, panic has set in. No matter that it is a common occurrence through forgetfulness, or poverty or Glasgow penny-pinching. Mammie is looking for bags of salt to throw on the fire: apparently, salt can douse flames. I used to wonder why Glasgow firemen didn't just have hoses that spouted salt! You don't buy bulk salt in case. So we get sent round the neighbours. 'Go and borrow salt from Mrs Macadam!' I always thought it was one up on the cup of sugar.

Children look on in awe and terror. Parents vainly hope that it will go out by itself and that there isn't a crack in the chimney to let the flames into the loft space. We are the centre of attention. The 'hingy-oot' becomes compulsory. It's akin to a street fight when the pubs come out. 'Come away in from there.' 'But I want to see the fire brigade!'

Some chimney fires are mere sparks that come and go to the great disappointment of onlookers. But some seem to improve as time goes on and the panic inside the house rises to hysteria. And eventually the fire brigade comes. The firemen come in quickly with their black uniforms and big rubber thigh-boots flapping. They put down a canvas on the floor and ask everyone to get out of the way. The hose comes in and goes up the chimney. Other firemen go up the stairs to see the roof and the loft. Outside the fire engine waits, its pumps going, and now surrounded by children, some mothers at their close-mouths, teddy boys appearing disinterested.

The kitchen fills with steam, soot and stoor. The embers come crashing down. The firemen have a cup of tea while it all cools down and wait to see if it is safe. My mother knows them and is embarrassed. She was a firewoman.

They go and the smell lingers. Now just recriminations. Bedclothes, curtains, outdoor clothes reeking, a fine black stoor covering everything, a cold fireplace. And everywhere a bitter, biting smell that will linger on for months.

And for a fact, hitherto unknown by me, my friend Henry tells me that around Fir Park, the (rest) home of Partick Thistle there always seemed to be a chimney on fire during a home game. This gave rise to the term 'Thistle lums'. Sounds painful.

The Cheapside Street Fire

I can't remember how we first got to know about it, but it was just at the beginning. The shouts went round that there was a fire in Cheapside Street. Now fires were quite common in the centre of Glasgow in the 1950s and '60s, common enough for us to look forward to them in a warped sort of way. We had seen the St Patrick's Girls School on fire as well as the famous St Andrew's Halls. These were enormous. The stables at the back of The Gaiety burned down and the smell of burning hay stayed for weeks. And lum fires and chip-pan fires were common, particularly on a Friday.

We went to see what was happening and at that stage as the first of the fire engines were arriving we could wander down Cheapside Street and Warroch Street to get a better view. To begin with, the fire was within the warehouse, which turned out to be a whisky bond owned by Arbuckle Smith and Co. There was not much to see, just the plumes of dark smoke, the smell of burning, the fire bells and the firemen running around, attaching hoses, just ignoring all those people who were in the way. In those days you could get very close to a fire and we all did that day.

The fire progressed and fire vehicles arrived in convoys. We went home for our teas but we were anxious to get out again. And when we did, the fire was getting bigger. We waited for hours as it got worse and the flames got higher. We could see down Cheapside Street, where there was a lot of activity. A fire engine had gone down the street and we could see it with its ladders extended high above the blaze with the hose having little impact on the fire below which was shooting higher.

There was a rumble and all of a sudden the fireman on the ladder wasn't there. A wall had come down and all we could see were clouds of dust and flames. The wall had completely engulfed the fire engine and the men in and around it. Except for the sound of burning and sudden gasps, there was complete silence. The memory of it has stayed with me ever since. I had just turned ten the day before and the fire was on Monday 28 March 1960.

We had to go to bed eventually but before we did, not that we could sleep, we went up to our flat roof where we could see the fire. I remember seeing flames higher than the church steeple nearby. My Auntie Polly in Nitshill said that they could see the flames from there, which must have been a good ten miles away.

I still remember the smell of whisky burning during the fire, which raged for three days killing fourteen firemen and five men of the Glasgow Salvage Corps. 300 firemen attended the fire as well as forty machines. It was the biggest peace-time fire in Glasgow's history.

And now I have a confession to make. Two days afterwards, the fire was still being doused with water from hoses snaking down Cheapside Street and Warroch Street. I was standing watching the firemen from the top of the joint of one of the hoses when it suddenly came apart, sending me flying and covering me with water. Before I fled the scene I could see in the distance one fireman's jet of water suddenly dying.

My mother had been a firewoman during the war and she knew a number of the men who were killed that day and night. Shops immediately set up funds for the families.

The Cheapside Street Fire.

If you can say that anything good could come of such an event it is that the whisky industry took notice and there has never been a repeat of such a fire in any distillery or bonded warehouse in Scotland. While no one can be certain, it is conjectured that the fire was started when highly inflammable whisky fumes came into contact with bare electric bulbs at the top of the warehouse. This should not now happen because of the health and safety measures put in place over the past years.

Short Back and Sides and Short Scratchy Trousers

My mother often said that I looked like a 'Pitt Street Modeler'. (Pitt Street had one of the 'Model' lodging houses referred to earlier.) This is because I: (a) looked like a bag tied in the middle or (b) something the cat dragged in. I certainly don't remember even bothering about my sartorial elegance in those days, maybe not even now.

However, standards must be maintained, and he of the Brylcreem slick-back and hard-polished shoes would pack me off, sometimes with my elder brother, for a haircut at Dick Carroll's. This was the sort of haircut that made your head freeze whenever you left the barber's and was probably the only reason we suffered those little school 'bunnets' at that time.

Dick Carroll had his barber shop in Argyle Street just up from Elderslie Street and round from Dover Street where Mr Connolly, 'The Big Yin', lived at one young time.

I do remember it being a sort of a back shop, and actually very well lit, which was a confidence booster with scissors flying around. You went in through a narrow corridor past cardboard signs for Brylcreem, Gillette and other razors and forgotten balms and shaving paraphernalia.

Those were the days when barbers shaved. It is coming back now, I am glad to say, with the influx of foreign barbers. In the small shop were two wooden barber's chairs, for all the world like two American electric chairs that you see in the movies e.g. *The Green Mile* with Tom Hanks which was a… I digress.

If you were as little as I was when I was young, he would put you on a board which he put across the arms of the chair so that you could be at his height for shearing. On the wall beside the door was a copper tea urn on a gas ring. In this urn he would steam towels for application to the 'mugs' of those who he would shave, slapping the towel on the mug and winding it round. It was fascinating to watch.

'What is a gas ring?' an early reader has asked me. Well, it was a simple cast-iron beast of an annular appearance (like a doughnut) with a pokey-out bit, actually a bit like a black cast-iron tennis racket. Out of the pokey-out bit would be a rubber pipe which would fit onto a gas pipe. One side of the doughnut would have holes from which gas would escape when a valve was turned on the pipe. You would then light the gas with a match. This was used under boilers such as the above, kettles at the back of offices and Dr Maguire had one in his surgery in which, as well as boiling his eggs, he also used to sterilise his scalpel before minor surgery such as verruca removal, verrucas being named after a volcano in Italy, no?

When I say that we went into the barber's, I have to say that with a shamed expression. Actually we went along the other side of Argyle Street to see if we could peer through to Dick's and if we could see someone in the chair then you would be sure that there was one person there and if you were lucky there might be someone else waiting.

You were lucky because Dick Carroll's seating, which was simply wooden benches ranged round two sides of the 'salon', had on them a pile of dirty magazines. 'Aidez-moi, Robert!' (or help ma Boab!). Yes, but not really in the same league that you get now (I suppose). There was *Titbits* and *Parade*. These magazines ensured that gentlemen kept their hair short and neat. I wondered about the nearly baldy ones who were there all the time. Anyway, *Titbits* and *Parade* were magazines with jokes, wee stories and lots of ladies, enough to excite the loins of a little chap like me. It wasn't for the cartoons alone I picked up those magazines with longing.

I always wondered why my father sent us there as he himself went, as did many other good citizens and Catholics. There we could read and see things that we would never get in Ireland's Own.

So, haircut achieved what now? Ah, suiting. You know, we were substantially and fairly elegantly clothed as youngsters and I believe that a great deal of effort was expended in that area to try and make us presentable. Still a lost cause.

We had, in those days, a strange system of purchasing expensive things. This was called 'getting a line' for a warehouse. Purchasing was strictly separated between retail and wholesale and you couldn't simply walk off the street into a wholesale warehouse and purchase something. However, if you had a contact on the inside, you could get a line which was basically a ticket to allow you to purchase the required. I remember that there was a lot of secrecy about this and you had to keep a low profile in case your entitlement to the line was questioned and you were thrown out.

Anyway, there were a number of these wholesale warehouses, mostly in what is now called Merchant City. One such was Bremners which I think was visited often. My memorable purchase was my first suit in real Harris Tweed. I think my mother had a thing about Harris Tweed as I wore it a lot.

The problem was that, being my very first suit, I was not yet at the age at which it was respectable to be in long trousers. (How this decision was reached I can't remember.) So, what was purchased for me was a rather Bertie Wooster, trendy for its time, Harris Tweed suit with short trousers.

Quality is on the march

In these stimulating and exhilarating days of the 1960's, with tremendous, high-speed technical activity in research and production, every hour sees some new discovery, some improvement in design and method of production. Quality is on the march. In all this, R. W. Forsyth's are somewhere up in front in the matter of clothes and footwear for men and women. Here, in every season of the year, will be found first-class apparel in wool, silk, cotton and in man-made fibres completely in tune with prevailing trends and styles : plus that intangible that adds to the pleasure of living—friendly, helpful service.

R. W. FORSYTH

R. W. Forsyth Ltd. Renfield Street Glasgow   CENtral 6271   And at Edinburgh

'You're looking awfae swanky like a dumpling in a hankie.'

SCHOOLWEAR FOR ALL AGES FROM PAISLEYS

Parents who care about the appearance of their children look to Paisleys for complete school outfitting, as their parents and grandparents have before them.

OFFICIAL OUTFITTERS
TO
ST. MUNGO'S ACADEMY
F.P. ASSOCIATION

PAISLEYS

PAISLEYS LIMITED,   JAMAICA STREET,   GLASGOW, C.1.   Tel: CITy 7811

The problem was that while certain parts were lined, the hems were not and I ended up with red scratchy rings round my legs and my parts suffered equally. Given the expense of these trousers and the efforts gone to to get them, including fitting, I was reluctant (i.e. scared) to make too much of it and so I suffered these deprivations secretly until it was time to move into longs.

And the time came to buy one's own suit and this was a right of passage for the teenager in Glasgow. Getting measured up for a suit was an expected part of the ritual. Our local tailor in Argyle Street (I can't remember his name, so come on, don't let me down) was the one to do so – and I cannot forget his question and the complete bewilderment (a facial expression I was quite good at, by the way) it caused: 'what way do you dress, sir?' Why can't they just put it clearly and not embarrass a young lad? It's akin to the barber asking you if you want something for the weekend: what, like a match ticket?

Cinemas and Heroes

Isn't it amazing that a few words said in a black and white movie forty years ago can still conjure up the image and smell of the cinema? Cinemas had their own smell and so did The Gaiety. We all had our local cinema to which we were loyal. The Gaiety was ours. This did not mean that we didn't wander out of our territory braving the 'gangs'. In Finnieston was The Kelvin with its colourful night-time side montages of the Souk, large minarets and walls and on the screen at the start always a boat in the sea and back-lit with blue and red muted lighting giving an air of the exotic East. The safety curtain had a large picture of a sailing boat in the distance and to accompany it, 'Red Sails in the Sunset' was sung by Nat King Cole (I think):

Red sails in the sunset,
Way out in the sea,
Carry my true love,
Home safely to me.

We wandered to The Tivoli in Crow Road besides Ross's ice-cream factory, the best ice cream ever. There we saw *Thunderball* and *The Parent Trap* with Hayley Mills and Maureen O'Hara.

Then there was the ABC Coliseum Cinerama which drew us over the Clyde. These were the experimental three-screen wide films of which very few were ever made. I saw *Ice Station Zebra* with Patrick McGoohan and *Krakatoa, East of Java*.

But back to The Gaiety. You queue up and defend your place, a balance between prudence and avoiding the bigger boys making fun of you or worse. You get your ticket and almost run through the foyer. Immediately you hit the cinema smell. The Gaiety was not unpleasant. There was always a strong smell of disinfectant and polish in the foyer.

Regarding 'foyer' – while Glaswegians are pretty down-to-earth, they seem to be quite happy to accept exotic French words when applied to cinemas. Greens Playhouse where the school took us to see *The Nun's Story* and *Ben Hur* had banquettes as well as a foyer! I don't think I ever went to a banquette and I'm not entirely sure about its uses.

Anyway, you get your seat and start shouting in anticipation. At Saturday afternoon matinees this was obligatory while waiting for the film to come on. You have to have your favourite seat. Mine was chosen by hard experience. Not too far back where the hard cases went and not under the balcony after the experience of my mother removing a great gob of chewing gum from my hair.

There is pandemonium until the lights go down and the film starts with an enormous banging of feet, the usherettes trying uselessly to quieten people down, threatening them with being thrown out and or barred. 'You're on yer last warning, ya wee shite.'

The noise grows in intensity as the film gets under way and it now occurs to me to ask why they bothered with soundtracks during matinees, because during the action you couldn't hear anything for the shouting and feet stomping. During the sissy bits you couldn't hear anything because of the booing and hissing and the fights breaking out.

British submarines would narrowly miss getting depth charged. Jack Hawkins would say, 'very good Number One, carry on.' Bing Crosby and Bob Hope would make us laugh all the way to Hong Kong. John Wayne would jump off of his horse on to an out-of-control Wells Fargo Stagecoach, kill a few Indians while driving eight horses and calmly save the lady. James Cagney would come screaming round a Chicago street corner in a limo, killing a few gangsters with a 'Tommy gun'. Then it was finished, except in those times you could sometimes sit through it all again. They had 'A' and 'B' pictures then and no one seemed to bother about payment as they didn't know when you came in.

Finished. Into the streets to continue playing cowboys and Indians or gangsters, where every one of them seemed to be called 'Joe', and if they were shot, were only shot in the shoulder. We played 'best falls' off dykes and walls, pretending to be shot. We got points for the best dramatic effect, similar to the way footballers behave now when they get a wee bump on the metatarsal or whatever part of the body is in vogue.

And at this time I have to confess to my children that I did dress as Davy Crockett, the American frontiersman, grabbed my Winchester and went into Argyle Street looking for 'bar'. However, in mitigation, around the age of ten, many others amongst my peers were also dressing as Davy Crockett. This, of course, was also the time of Robin Hood and William Tell but the thought of dressing up in green tights on the streets of Anderston was a no-no.

Davy, Davy Crockett
King of the wild frontier
Born on a mountaintop in Tennessee
Killed a 'bar when he was only three
Davy, Davy Crockett
King of the wild frontier.

Then chips. It seemed to be compulsory after the pictures. Stout fat chips covered in vinegar and sometimes a pickle. Then home to dream of cowboys and Corvettes. 'Make smoke number one.' 'Hoist the mainsail, Mr Christian.'

At this point I have to have a quiet word about usherettes. They were the mainstay of the cinema, the barrier between fun and mayhem. The guardians of regular queues, the pitie-ooter if there was trouble, the help to find your lost shoe at the end (don't even ask).

It's not the function. It's the word. I have long wondered where we got the 'ette' from in Glasgow, as it does seem to be peculiar to the Dear Green Place. Can you just image Annette in the kitchenette with a serviette? When did a napkin become a serviette? When did a 'scullery' become a kitchenette? And what about Jeanette in the dinette? Is that a little dining room? When did a laundry become a launderette? And most of all when new flats in Anderston started to appear; some of them were on two floors and were called 'maisonettes'. Pretentious – moi?

Skinny malinky long legs
Big banana feet
Went to the pictures and couldnae get a seat
When the picture started
Skinny malinky farted
Skinny malinky long legs big banana feet... (You couldn't make it up!)

'Do you work at Bilslands?'

More Entertainment By the Way

I started off this book by referring to the 1950s and '60s as being black and white, but on reflection we had a whale of a time and it is a wonder that we found any time to go to school because we were always doing something and there was always something to do.

And school was an entertainment. I do not know to this day if it was particular to Catholic schools but I suppose the standards must have applied even in the Proddy schools (for that is what they were called). Our education in what could have been considered a run-down area was superb. At primary school we were introduced to classical music by way of big loudspeakers that we were sent to collect from the school office. These were then plugged into a little socket on the wall and we were told to be completely silent while we listened to classical music. We had violin lessons and piano lessons at school and were taken to concerts at the St Andrews Halls.

St Andrews Halls burned down around 1963 and, to our surprise, our cinema, The Gaiety, which had just closed, was taken over as the new, temporary Glasgow Concert Hall and it was redecorated. We were among the first people to see it when the Glasgow schools were treated to Benjamin Britten's *A Young Persons' Guide to the Orchestra* conducted by the famous Scottish conductor Sir Alexander Gibson. It was really strange to see The Gaiety with full lights on and splendidly painted.

Now the concert hall was the venue for a wide range of acts in the 1960s, among them the Beatles and the Dubliners, with whom I drank Guinness in my very early and under-age drinking days in The Shandon Bells. The Shandon Bells is now known as The Buttery, which was originally the posh restaurant to the rear of the pub. In those days it had a great bar at the front where you got the best roast-beef sandwich in Glasgow.

The Shandon Bells is just over the road from where the Glasgow Concert Hall was and it was the first port of call for artists who mixed well with the locals. One night, the famous André Previn was conducting an orchestra and during the interlude popped over for a libation. Standing at the bar next to him was a couthy local who eyed him carefully and said, 'you look familiar pal. Do you work at Bilslands?'

Back to school where we would see films on the old 35mm projector which would be set up in a classroom where we would be seated and told to be quiet while the teacher threaded the film and then the blackout curtains would be drawn and we would be shown a wide variety of films. Regulars were Walt Disney nature films like the story of a salmon making its way from the sea up the river to spawn (although the teacher would never mention that word, by the way).

I remember seeing John Grierson's *The Night Mail* with words by W.H. Auden. This was made for the Post Office Film Unit. We were also taken to see selected films of a religious nature. We were taken, teachers, nuns as well as girls from St Patrick's Girls School to see *Ben Hur* and *The Nun's Story*, both in Green's Playhouse which was to go on to become the famous Apollo. Sometimes we were taken to the Glasgow Art Galleries for exhibitions and films and I particularly remember seeing Lawrence Olivier in *King Richard III* there.

At Christmas time there was the parade down Argyle Street of the circus on its way to the Kelvin Hall with all the trimmings – clowns, acrobats, fire-eaters and jugglers, and that was just the people coming out of the pubs to watch! We would go and see the switching on of the Christmas lights at George Square and walk down Buchanan Street where all the shops were done up for Christmas. But particularly it was brilliant to go and see the model trains going round the charity Christmas tree in the Central Station.

Actually there was a brilliant machine in the Central Station and most big stations had them. This was a big red machine about 3ft high with a slanting top on which was a big dial. For pennies, you could punch out a long aluminium strip with your name (or your dog's name on it). I suppose these were intended for traveller's bags but were mostly used by wee boys like me and we never got the names right anyway and if your name was Peter Fitzpatrick or Gerry McLaughlin you gave up before you started.

There were the pantomimes, of course, that we normally went to see in The Alhambra with stars such as Rikki Fulton and Charlie Sim, or Jimmy Logan and Johnnie Beattie. We would also go and see the carnival at the Kelvin Hall which was fine but the best of all were the 'shows' where you could shoot down cans to win plaster dugs, go and see the bearded lady or play the numerous 'automatons', the machines where you put in a penny and a scene opened up in front of you, maybe a skeleton coming out of a coffin in a graveyard but I only remember them vaguely.

I do remember the story of the corporation councillors' visit to the carnival to inspect it. While they were there, they came across a corporation attendant taking a big brush with soap and water to clean an elephant's bottom. One councillor was very impressed with the obvious care that was being taken and asked the attendant why he was so careful. 'Well,' he said, 'someone has to do it and if a job is worth doing then it is worth doing properly.' Duly impressed, the councillor said so and also that he could put in a good word for the attendant as there were bound to be better jobs in the corporation where he could make a good impression. 'No thanks,' said the attendant, 'I'd rather stay in show business!' It was the same Glasgow councillor, by the way, who, when told that someone had made serious allegations against him, threatened to find out who the alligator was!

FESBs (see football) at Glasgow Art Gallery, 1950s.

GIFTS OF
MONEY, BOOKS
TOYS Etc.
WILL BE
DISTRIBUTED TO
LOCAL
HOSPITALS
AND RAILWAY AND
OTHER CHARITIES

Christmas tree in Central Station.

If you were not going to the pantomime with the Cubs, then you were rehearsing for the Scout Gang Show or the youth club show in the Parochial Halls. I remember well rehearsing my part in the girlie chorus for a popular song of that time sung by Johnny Ray, 'Walking My Baby Back Home'. We were politically incorrect and dressed up as Black and White Minstrels and sang 'Mammie'. We went to Glasgow Green and took part in bogie rallies with very sophisticated and decorated bogies (see bogies).

We gathered milk-bottle tops for some cause as well as the yearly Bob-a-Job. And, we went to Scout Camp. Actually, when I think about it, the summers were so long and seemed to go on forever. And some years we had three holidays. That sound posh but this is how it worked. In primary school we paid up to go to school camp. I believe that this was a successor to 'Fresh Air Fortnight' designed so that inner-city youths could experience the delights of the outside.

By the way, the expression, 'do you think it's Fresh Air Fortnight?' was commonly used in a pejorative way to remonstrate with those who had failed to close a door, thereby letting in the cooling draught.

Anyway, we would pay our weekly amount to Mr Seenan, and prepare for the camps which were actually in the classrooms of little schools throughout the country. We would holiday in far-flung places such as Ballantrae, Arbroath, Tarbet and Newton Stewart. I don't remember a lot about these holidays except the smell of army blankets and sanitised sawdust for the floors, food parcels from my father from home and getting not to go to Mass because the bus didn't turn up. 'You have not to worry about this,' said Mr Seenan. 'It is not a sin if you want to go and are prevented from doing so!' I often wondered if it was a mortal sin if you went to Mass but didn't really want to?

The whole idea of course was to allow those whose parents could not afford a holiday for their children a cheap way of doing it. I suppose it was also a great relief to pack us off for a while.

That reminds me of a summer camp run by the Co-op that my brother Jim went to and came back fighting fit and healthy. I think it was down near Ballantrae also but on that summer camp they forced the happy campers to wear balloons stuck to their legs while queuing for lunch. It must have been some sort of a punishment camp (pictured on page 67).

Back from school camp and we got ready for Scout Camp. These were different in that they were actually camps which were packed up and set up with military precision. My first camp was to Arklow in Ireland, and every two years we made a foray to Torquay. Besides the everlasting warm summers, what I remember most was the travel to camp, overnight on a steam train to London, changing at Crewe or Newcastle. I would spend a great deal of the time hanging out of the train window getting covered in soot although I never noticed until it got into my eye.

We travelled overnight without berths and slept where we could. Some (thin) people slept in the overhead luggage racks, taking the bulbs out so that it would be darker. There were card schools for the older ones or we simply walked up and down the long corridor trains till, tired and mucky, we would arrive in London to transfer to the train to Torquay where we would arrive to be transported to camp on an open lorry, arriving just in time for lunch made by the advance party sent on to build the camp.

This photograph reminds me of one incident at camp in which Mick Green, the chap with the mouth organ (in photograph on page 68), figured prominently. Some forgotten chap was having an altercation with Mick Rankin and the said bold Rankin was quick to get off his mark and make an escape. The forgotten chap unfortunately had a very bad lisp and called out just as Mick Green hove into view round a tent towards which was running the hapless Rankin: 'Hey Gween – stop Wan….' The Rankin chase was forgotten as the indignant Gween took up the altercation with the said lisper. Others appearing in the photograph are Brian Caulfield with Fair Isle and Jim McGinnis in the middle. I've forgotten the names of the others.

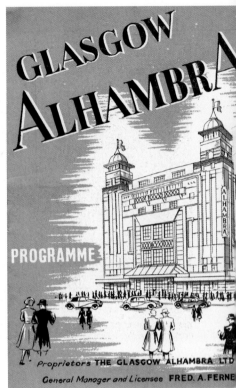

Above left and right: Johnnie Beattie, and the Alhambra.

And back to more holidays, because once you got back from camp you might go with your parents 'doon the water' to Innellan or Dunoon. One particular time we had gone to Girvan for a very wet fortnight and while I don't remember a great deal about it I do remember my big brother Martin coming home early from Scout Camp in Torquay and turning up off the train wearing short socks, a kilt and sailor top and carrying a tartan kitbag! It turned out that the whole troop had been on an outing and had returned to camp to see in the distance an oblong smouldering patch where once had been a large tent.

The tent had gone on fire and no one knew how. The only clothes that the inhabitants had were those that they were standing up in. Some passing sailor had kindly donated the natty white top with a blue trim. Maybe it was a Sea Scout, I don't remember. Anyway, having no clothes and no holiday home, the unfortunate campers were packed off home – or in his case, to Girvan.

Now I do remember the red radio. This of course was in the great days of doing things at home of a hobby nature, like making ships out of matches or putting ships into bottles, even ships made of matches into bottles?

My father was a physics teacher and a dab hand at electric things. So when the first transistor radios came along he was among the first to have a go at sending off and putting the kit together at the kitchen table. I do remember him working away at it to get it ready for Martin to take away on Scout Camp. And it did work and Martin was the only Scout to have such a novelty.

Unfortunately, it was a victim of the conflagration. On return, searching about the remains, there it was, a frizzled-up blob of red plastic and wires – gone. Tears were shed but there was a strange ending to the story. A certain amount of insurance was shared out between the victims of the Great Torquay Tent Fire but on relating this story to the Man from the Prudential, he opined

Brother Jim, second from the left (note the FESB on the far right).

that there might be a small claim in this. In fact, he found out that we were well covered for the destruction of our holiday home! This of course covered the cost of a replacement transistor radio. Strangely though, my dad didn't seem up for making another one.

Of course, summer camps and summer holidays were not the end of it as we went many weekends to Scout Camp at Auchengillan, north of Glasgow and near Drymen, where the historic wee Hutters of Carbeth gallantly resist the raising of rents by the landowners.

Our preparations for weekend camp generally started the week before when lists of provisions were doled out to everyone. Now you might be allowed to think that being Scouts, we would be eating healthily off the land, with steaks cooked over an open fire and garnished with wild berries from the hill and mushrooms picked in the morning dew. 'Damn the fear of it!', as they used to say. In fact what actually happened was that each young lad was requested to bring a tin of meat and possibly a packet of Smash as well as maybe a packet of custard and a tin of fruit. (Smash was dried potato which was reconstituted with water. It was much loved in the 1960s.)

The tins of meat would be opened up and generally put into one 'dixie' to be heated up. Unfortunately some mothers would have a liberal definition of the term 'meat' and you would find yourself eating a combination of corned beef and mince garnished with almost-liquid mashed potatoes because someone had put too much liquid into the Smash.

This could be followed by burnt custard and anything. I remember one torturous weekend at Auchengillan, the Glasgow Scout Camp: we had arrived and pitched our tents in a grey mist which stayed for two whole days. My brother Martin and I were sharing a small two-man bivouac and there were two other larger tents. My brother had the flu and was ill and uncommunicative for two days and feverish in the night. The only alternative was one of the larger tents where everyone else had gathered in a circle to fart and tell dirty jokes and sing dirty songs and at one stage they passed round, as if it were a ritual, a large ten-pint aluminium dixie full of pink Creamola Foam. I am afraid the thought of it now gives me the boak.

On the way to Scout camp in Torquay.

Television

I don't remember when I saw my first TV programme, but as for many others, it was to change Glaswegians' lives forever. I do remember the debates about whether TV would ruin our eyes, make us unfit and otherwise contaminate our young lives. On reflection, maybe it did?

And apologies to my son, who has been castigated many a time by me for poking his fingers into places both dangerous and embarrassing. 'Would you take your son out of here please?' would be heard occasionally. There was, of course, the time in the tourist office in the old water tank thingy in Perth. There we were, alone in this large rotunda with about three synchronised slide projectors putting on a show round the inside of the domed roof. While we were looking upwards, the son wandered round behind a counter and obviously poked something on the projectors which started to whirr ominously and produced a show at triple speed.

Rather than hang on and explain yet again, we hared it out of there and, in one of our many family quotes, 'I have never been so angry.'

Well anyway, the reason for my apology is that on the first exposure to me of the brand new cabinet TV set at my Auntie Peggy's, I went round the back and twiddled knobs which spoiled the party, first of all because I was supposed to be playing musical chairs and secondly, I had produced on the TV screen a series of black and white bars which could not be sorted except by 'getting a man in.' Tempers were lost. Ears were boxed. Curiosity and fiddling with all things electronic is possibly inherited.

Because, in those days, TVs were temperamental and would go off if you looked at them. We had one which you could only see if you taped a stick to the top and placed a newspaper on the stick so that the light wouldn't get on to the screen. Sometimes you had to watch in complete darkness and I remember friends of ours, the Caulfields, had a TV that you could only watch

A proprietary version of the stick and paper.

John Grierson in *This Wonderful World*.

in darkness and in order to see the screen, they had a thing like a huge magnifying glass on the screen. It was a bit peculiar walking into people's houses in complete darkness with only the flickering screen in the corner. 'Is that you, Michael?'

TV was brilliant. I would rush home at lunchtime from school to see the start of the *One O'Clock Gang*. This was about the first lunchtime 'Magazine show'. It was hosted by Larry Marshall and featured such prominent Scottish stars as Ricky Fulton and Charlie Sim, who did a regular classroom skit. There was the Peggy O'Keefe Trio and Johnnie Beattie. On one tremendous occasion I actually got to be in the television audience. At that age, that beat everything. That might actually have been the show with an appearance from Michael Holliday, the singer of the famous 'The Story of my Life' as well as 'The Runaway Train' (came over the hill). Sadly Michael died of a suspected self-administered drugs overdose in 1963, at a time when his career seemed on the downward slope. There was Bill Tennent, one of the first ever newsreaders and presenters.

My other all-time favourite programme was *This Wonderful World* hosted by the great John Grierson. This programme, in black and white, featured short films and animations from throughout the world, and as far as I can remember, was the only one to do so until the concept was reintroduced by Bob Harris in *The Old Grey Whistle Test* in the 1970s. The programme was innovative and enjoyable and started me on a lifetime love of documentary.

Enjoy your viewing tonight with the T.V. guide.

Charlie Sim.

Larry Marshall.

Michael O'Hallaran.

Bill Tennent.

I did not know at that time about the importance of John Grierson but he was instrumental in many ways in making documentaries an art form. He was responsible for the ground-breaking film of the Scottish fishing fleet, *Drifters,* and also *The Night Mail*, which had a script by W.H. Auden and a musical score by Benjamin Britten. He was instrumental in setting up the Post Office Film Unit as well the National Film Board of Canada. It is a credit to STV that they saw the potential for showing such experimental works as they did on *This Wonderful World*.

And who can forget the voice of Michael O'Hallaran welcoming us to 'Scottish Television broadcasting from the Blackhill Transmitter of the Independent Television Authority'? Of course there was always *Look*, the safari programme with Armand and Michaela Denis. (How do I remember these things?) There was Johnny Morris who took the voices of animals and of course there were the first quiz shows – *Take your Pick* with Michael Miles and *Double your Money* with Hughie Green.

Wan Singer, Wan Song

Before I go on to talk about songs and singing I have to just share with you a strange thing that I recently discovered to my horror and I have put the photo of the cover in here to prove to you the truth because otherwise you would not believe me. It is of Danny Kaye (he of Hans Christian Anderson fame and the chalice in the palace – look it up) singing 'I Belong to Glasgow' live in New York. And I have to tell you that it is truly awful. I believe that Danny Kaye did appear at the Glasgow Empire but that was before my time.

We lived to sing and sing we did at the drop of a hat. At weddings, funerals, Hogmanay, Christmas and at the very regular shows put on by youth clubs, churches, Scouts and school.

ANATOLE OF PARIS
I BELONG TO GLASGOW
TCHAIKOVSKY
GOOD OLD 149
BALLIN' THE JACK
TRIPLETS
THE PEONY BUSH
MANIC DEPRESSIVE PRESENTS
I'VE GOT A
LOVELY BUNCH OF
COCONUTS

'It wid gie ye the boak.'

My very first experience of singing in public was the never-to-be-repeated, once-in-a-lifetime singsong at school camp in Newton Stewart. There in the big new school gymnasium with pupils all round the walls, I was given a song sheet of 'Tom Dooley' as in 'Hang Down yir Heed'. I was propelled by some sadist into the middle of the hall and told to sing. This may have been a mix-up in that they possibly thought that I even knew what a Tom Dooley was, let alone sing about it. Anyway, the word is 'corpsed': although I had the words there in front of me, without the least inkling of a tune I floundered. However, pretending to be Caruso I plodded on starting into the first verse with the first tune that came into my head, which I think was 'On Top of Old Smoky' which I thought was very similar. However, the virtual big hook came out and I was propelled back to the bench at the edge of the gym suffering the slings and arrows of those unforgiving big boys.

It was no mix-up! I was always pretty sure it was the big boys getting me back for clyping them for smoking and playing brag in the lavvies. 'See wee Meighan sir, he's just a dab hand at singing Tom Dooley. He'll do a good show.'

Anyway while it may have put me off singing on my own in front of others (for a while anyway), it did not put me off singing or songs. Of course, coming from a good Irish God-fearing Catholic background it behoved us to know the words of several hundred Irish rebel songs which we sung with gusto, particularly on bus runs on the way to rallies where, among other things, in full uniform we would repeat our allegiance to the Queen and to good Christian values!

The fact that we sang about Kevin Barry being shot in a chair or tortured by the bad Protestant bastards didn't seem to conflict with these stoutly-held Christian Scouting principles. It must have been a cultural thing for sure but on the other hand I liked nothing better to than get along to Argyle Street or Sauchiehall Street to see and hear a good old Orange walk and in fact, the Ould Orange Flute became a firm favourite of mine.

The expression, 'wan singer, wan song' could often be heard at Hogmanay parties as each one in time round the kitchen would give of his best rendition of 'Danny Boy' or 'The Mountains of Mourne', which was my dad's favourite. While I remember, he also had a hideous tie of that same venue, or was it the Lakes of Killarney? Anyway he did go in for neckpieces then with panoramic vistas, but never actually wore them.

What always amazed me was that at parties, grown men who would never want to let it be known that they were sentimental would sing wistfully of taking 'Kathleen home again' or 'it was only a shanty, in old shanty town, its roof is so slanty it touches the ground'. Of course the only problem here was that you had to sing without the Glasgow dialect as you couldn't very well sing about 'shanty toons' and 'touching the grun.' It just wouldn't rhyme. Therefore, Glaswegian crooners would tend to put on their best voices and give laldy to such poetic gems as 'San Francisco'.

But tell me, how is it that very nearly 100 per cent of Glaswegians who would sing about the loneliness of Paris, the glory that was Rome or going home to the city by the Bay, had never actually been there? Going to Rothesay, yes, or Saltcoeetes would be understandable, but the strange affiliation with the West Coast of America was always very strange to me.

We sang at Cubs and Scouts, some songs which were very stirring like 'Faith of our Fathers' or equally some strange songs more akin to what would be sung in rugby clubs – but we won't go into that. We sang carols at Christmas and when the teachers weren't there we sang: 'Three wee kings of Orient are, selling knickers in George's Square, very fantastic, no elastic, buy them for the fair.'

There were Glasgow favourites such as Glen Daly and I am sure that his album 'Live at the Ashfield Club' must have been in the album charts before the Beatles. So too was Sidney Devine, not a great favourite of mine but others loved him. I saw Glen Daly at our school show once and he was good and he could sing 'San Francisco' with the best of them.

We were visited at school once by the late great Father Sydney MacEwan who didn't sing for us but played 'I'll Take you Home Again Kathleen' from his 'Best of' album. I think that he had actually come to our school hall to talk to us about the missionaries and the Black Babies, because they were always coming to talk to us about the Black Babies and the propagation of the faith, and here, most of us would not have a clue, just wanting to stand up off the prickly hard coconut mats which were eating into us and producing rashes on our bodies. Later on though, I

got to appreciate the singing of the great Irish tenors such as himself, Joseph Locke and John McCormack.

At concerts we sang about 'westering home with a song in the air' or about 'Nut Brown Maidens', whatever they were. And of course at Hogmanay we all tried to sing 'Auld Lang Syne' but nobody ever knew the words.

Cranstonhill Baths and washing house.

Cranstonhill Baffs

I suppose everyone has a favourite place in their youth and in their home town. Mine is Cranstonhill and I'll tell you why in a minute: it's not that I don't like other places which were brilliant in my youth like Kelvingrove Park and Rouken Glen and Central Station, but for some reason Cranstonhill Baths stick in my mind.

Cranstonhill is between Anderston and Finnieston if not overlapping (for the argumentative Glaswegians sitting in pubs who might debate the point for an hour – 'Aye, it wis.' 'No, it wisnae.' 'Ach, yer arse in parsley, it wis.' 'Yir bum's oot the windae, it wisnae'. 'See you, you're no wise.'

From Argyle Street you would walk up the hill on your way to the local leisure centre, only in those days we called it 'The Baths'. You would pass the Prince of Wales pub. I remember it as being a highly polished long bar with that Glasgow beery smell mixed with tobacco but also polish. I say this as it was expected that you would have a look into pubs on your way past sometimes and often the doors were open. Apparently that was against the law as it was illegal for children to be able to see people drinking in a pub: that's why they had such high windows. (If you have a look at The Buttery, which used to be called 'The Shandon Bells', you will see a spy hole to allow the local constabulary to look in. This was quite common in pubs – and incidentally, banks used to have iron steps set into the walls to allow the constabulary to peer in to see that all was well in the banking world.)

You would wander up Hydepark Street past the Milanda Bakery where you'd get the smell of freshly baked bread and morning rolls, the pigeons swarming at the smell and fighting for the crumbs. Past the fire station where you could peek in and see the firemen cleaning their hoses. Smell the canvas and leather and polish. Although my mother left the National Fire Service before I was born, she still had friends in the service and we would occasionally visit there. And finally, into The Baths, where the boys were strictly segregated from the girls; The Baths were crowded. Boys were jumping from 'the dale' and whistles were blowing. No one seemed to swim in those days, we just splashed. In fact, it was many years before I could swim. We just had fun and such was the bureaucracy that we had to either dress and go to the front door to pay again if we wanted another 'go'. None of your fancy armbands then.

You had had enough, so into the changing boxes ranged around the pool, flicking towels at your pals. Then to the Brylcreem machine beside the door to lather your hair in the slicked-back style of the 1950s. We were looking for 'The Brylcreem Bounce'. Saying that, my father used Brylcreem all of his life and then used the tubs for keeping nails and things.

Brylcreem
A little dab'll do ya!
Brylcreem
You'll look so debonair
Brylcreem
The gall's all pursue ya
They'll love to get their fingers in your hair.

(As sung by Connie Francis and the Jordanaires)

Coming out you could take a side door through the 'Steamie' where the women did their weekly wash. I sometimes had to take our washing there done up in a great big bundle. You had to brave the cheek you got from the women washing using the great big machines and mangles: 'here, you son. Behave yourself. Dae yae think it's outside yer in?'

Spilling out of the door and over the street to the wee sweetie shop where you get a one penny or two-penny jar of ginger served up to you in an empty Shipham's fish paste jar and a 'poke' of sweets in a twist of newspaper. Then we would move on with our swimming 'trunks' over our heads like Arabs and whooped it up the whole way home, possibly pelting one another with our pea-shooters loaded with split peas or throwing bombs, those little plastic missiles in which you loaded caps, threw them up as far as you could and they came down to earth exploding on the pavement. Or we had blue potato guns which you pushed into a potato, breaking off a slug to be fired at anyone. Eyes were lost. 'See you Meighan: you're just a big diddie!' 'Aye right buggerlugs – yer arse in parsley.'

Of course, The Baths were of the old-fashioned type with the changing boxes ranged round the pool and the high, vaulted roofs like a church. These have either been refurbished or replaced with leisure centres. Some years ago, while working in Shotts, I stopped the car to enquire of two little boys (in the days when one could do that), 'can you tell me where the leisure centre is?' They looked at me in silence and doubt. I said, 'the swimming pool?' In unison their eyes lit up as they said, 'oh aye, Shotts Baffs! They're up the hill on the right!'

It was, as they had insinuated, 'baffs' of the reconstructed Victorian era in the last stages of their life, as told by the scruffy paintwork. These were soon to be replaced by the new type of leisure centre.

> If a bumbee stung a bumbee
> On the bumbee's bumbee,
> What colour would the bumbee's bum be?
> 'Bumbee tartan!'

The 48 Bus

In the 1950s and '60s, before one-man buses were introduced, bus conductors were more in evidence. In Glasgow in particular there was the 'clippie'. The conductors saw themselves as being very powerful and not to be trifled with.

Some of these conductors adopted a strange habit of wearing their money bags and ticket machines, 'The Ultimate', as far down their legs as possible, a bit like some Western 'gunslingers'. This meant that to get a ticket or change they had to pull the bag and the machine up by the leather straps, which were sometimes extended to add length, or lean down to reach them.

These conductors, with their low-slung bags and gruff language, gave a sometimes aggressive appearance and they often had the manners to go along with the appearance. 'Come on, get aff', is a well-known Glasgow pejorative.

One such busman, particularly 'hard-bitten', conducted the No. 48 bus one Saturday afternoon when it was full of passengers on the way to Nitshill. Now, in those days most buses were built in such a way that you would enter at the open back end, where there was a platform dominated by the ' clippie'. Over the Jamaica Bridge and beside the Cinerama, the bus stopped at the lights and as it stopped a man started to get off. The clippie said, 'this isnae a stop, pal'. 'So what!' said the man as he jumped, 'I'm aff anyway.' 'You're aff your heed, you mean,' shouted the clippie, at which the man, now on the pavement, made a rude gesture and shouted loudly at the conductor, 'you're nothing but a wee ★ ★ ★ dictator.'

The conductor had had enough. Taking off his machine and bag he shoved them into his wee cupboard under the stairs and jumped off the bus after the man who had so insulted him and damaged his hard-won status and respect. Blows were exchanged before the passenger turned and fled, hotly pursued by the conductor who chased him along the street and round a corner.

No. 4 to Drumoyne. (Catriona Meighan)

All of this was taking place out of sight of the driver and the bus started off without the conductor. It went several stops before the driver realised that the cacophony of bells ringing were the wee old wifies shouting: 'Hey son, ye've lost yer clippie!' Unfortunately, on being asked by the perplexed driver, none of us could tell what happened to his conductor and from that day to this I have wondered.

My father told me of one such female conductor on a bus in Duke Street who was urging a fellow teacher to kindly and quickly vacate the platform. When informed by the very proper and dignified passenger that she was being rather bombastic, she threatened to report him to the police for swearing at her: 'Did youse hear that? He called me a ★ ★ ★.'

That also reminds me of the nice Glasgow lad who fell into a cement mixer and came out a wee hard man!

And a final word about the fine advanced driving skills of the Glasgow bus driver: it is a well-known fact that their interpretation of the use of signalling is that they do so to alert you to the fact that they have indeed pulled out and that they are now either in front of you or are forcing you into the middle of the road to be confronted by one of their colleagues now bearing down on you.

That reminds me of the customer-care skills of one highly-motivated and customer-focused driver in Argyle Street. While waiting at the bus stop, my bus came and went straight by me, as was often the case as being only 6ft 3in. I am fairly invisible.

Anyway, I saw that the bus was slowing down for the lights so I pursued the said bus with an indignant gait, hammering on the bus door. At this point the door opened and I was gratified to think that my remonstrations had had an immediate effect.

However his opening shot was: 'If you want this bus youse better stand at the right stop pal.' He then closed the door and pulled smartly away through the green lights. And so, not standing on dignity, I just had to walk home! 'Hingin's too good fur him!'

GSN 820 Our First Car

That was the number of our first car. Isn't it amazing how you can remember something like that? It must have been bought on the day President Kennedy was assassinated. Only joking, because that was a Friday and I was at the Scouts and it was on the news just before we went out.

It was a maroon and white Ford Consul and it was enormous. It gave us a lot of pleasure and a lot of pain. It was acquired just as we were about to move from our tenement and into the leafy glades in order to transport teacher and family to school in Townhead.

Prior to getting the car we either had to use Shank's pony or take the bus, tram or train. However, with the move it seemed logical although we didn't actually stay far from the station at Scotstounhill. I think it was more for ease of travel to far-flung football games in such exotic and out-of-the-way places as East Fife or Kilmarnock. It was also useful for days out, though I think that we may have borrowed a car from a pawnbroker friend of my father, and I am sure it is the car behind the Humber shown in the picture at the start of 'The Close'.

It was only the second car in the close, the first being Freddy Thomson's Triumph Mayflower. It wasn't new because we were not that posh – it was actually bought from the Auction Mart which took place in the cattle market in the Gallowgate when the cattle weren't there – but the smells were. I remember my father showing me the wooden machine at the Gallowgate that came down over a 'coos' neck in order to stun it before death. He promptly pulled my head back out before I did something stupid; this was of course, before foot-and-mouth, and men and beasts could freely mingle.

The vehicles on display were wide and varied, ranging from ex-police cars and old buses to military vehicles. It was brilliant to be able to climb in and out of them and watch them all being started up to test before the auction. I wasn't at the auction when our car was bought but my father turned up with the said Consul and there was nothing for it but to go for a wee run.

My father had originally been a motor mechanic and he kept that car in brilliant order, even taking out the gearbox and engine. I remember this because he explained to me what a micromesh gearbox was and showed what happened when the gears were crunched. Large parts of metal came off the gears and floated about the gearbox causing all sorts of problems. He looked after that car until the day it died somewhere in the east end. I carried out the last task of taking the log book to the garage where my father had been paid a fiver for the scrap. We moved on soon to a Ford Popular but that just wasn't as interesting.

Thinking about cars reminds me of a wee story about name droppers. Not that I am averse to mentioning the great and the good that I have met: in fact, at one time I was an advisor on alcohol consumption to both the Secretary of State for Scotland and to the great Mick McGahey, the then Secretary of the Scottish Miners' Union. They had both been attending the Scottish Trades Union Conference in the Douglas Hotel in Aberdeen and had come into the bar where I was working. 'What's your best beer?' said Mick. 'That would be your Tartan Special,' said I.

Anyway, name droppers. I lived in the Highlands and Islands for many years, near Dingwall to be exact. Now during that time, I got a call from Rankin to say that Tommy Dingwall had been invited to a reception and to watch Ross County play at Victoria Park. Now Tommy Dingwall was the Lord Provost of Glasgow and any Glaswegian knows that the Lord Provost travels in the famous, if not original, Glasgow Rolls Royce G1.

So, in due course, I, Tommy Dingwall, his wife Grace, chauffeur and two Men in Black aka Tam Fleming and Mick Rankin turned up at the Tulloch Castle Hotel for said reception. I am sure the good people of Ross County had no idea that the two bodyguards were both Celtic supporters and freeloaders and their only involvement with Glasgow City was their employment as teachers and friends of Tommy.

Rootes present a New Hillman— the SUPER MINX

★ Up to 80 m.p.h. from a 1.6 litre engine

★ Padded facia, dished steering wheel

★ Wide opening doors, outstanding passenger space and headroom

★ Only three greasing points!

PLUS built in heater, windscreen washers and safety belt anchor points at no extra cost.
Price **£854.7.3** (£585 plus p.t. £269.7.3)

Andersons
of Newton Mearns

Above: The Hillman Super Minx.

Right: 'Have you seen a wee boy?'

Anyway, a good time was had by all and I joined Rankin, Fleming, Tommy Dingwall and chauffeur for post-celebration drinks in the bar as well as breakfast in the hotel. Following a wee walk round Dingwall to see the canal, it was time for Tommy and entourage to set off. From the front of the National Hotel the Glasgow Rolls Royce, with flags flying, set off on its journey back to Glasgow.

At that point, a certain local worthy passed by and stopped. Looking wistfully at me saying 'bye' to The High Heid Yin from Glasgow, he said, 'I once met the Lord Provost of Stirling!'

This also reminds me of a friend who was driving along the Clydeside Expressway at too high a speed when he was stopped by a police motorcycle rider. 'Do you realise that you were doing over forty sir? What would you do if there was mist or fog about?' 'I would take mister foot off mister accelerator.' 'Step out of the car sir…'

Above: 'Ginger'.

Left: Church outings and travel by train.

A Day Out

Going 'Doon the Water' was for longer holidays. For days out there were lots of places: you could go to Hogganfield Loch and spend the day on the boating pond; you could go to Rouken Glen which was another Glasgow park and another adventure. In fact, you could spend your summer holidays simply going round the numerous Glasgow parks: Queen's Park with the musty Fossil Grove, King's Park where you could get a brilliant view of Glasgow from the flagpole. But best was going on the train to Helensburgh or Balloch, and sometimes Girvan.

The preparation was all. The big metal flask was prepared with tea with milk already in and the cork stopper wedged tightly in with a piece of cloth. The bread would be a Glasgow loaf with the thick crusts still on, ready for the banana. Boldly we would set out with our bottles of ginger up to Charing Cross station to get the steam train to Balloch: there we would make straight for the little beach at the end of Loch Lomond where the boatyard was and where we could see the *Maid of the Loch* at the pier. The smells of Balloch were not the smells of the sea but it had a sandy beach, it was hot and the water was clear.

Balloch Pier

A leathered hand rests
Upon the polished sill
And waives its option to produce thunder.
In the hot-oil smell and smoke
And for a moment only
Summer is caught in
Sweet and docile drowsiness
Power and quiet
Are here together
Captured for a moment
On Balloch Pier.

Of course, there were also the bus runs. We had bus runs at the drop of a hat. There were Scout and Cub bus runs, school bus runs, and bus runs for any occasion, such the company bus run pictured, which I think was to celebrate my father getting married. There was the pub bus run, which I was never on, but I do remember that The Gaiety Bar had a celebrated bus run that my father would look forward to and I believe that he may even have had a hand in organising.

There was always the mystery bus run that would set out from Killermont Street bus station to some unknown destination such as Callendar or Aberfoyle (although you didn't know that then, because it was a mystery), where it would wait for an hour or two before departing homewards.

I once had the stupidity to think that this was a good trip on which to invite a girl on an early date. She never turned up and that was a real mystery!

As Long as Ye've Got Yir Health

The National Health Service was in its infancy in the 1950s, although we did not realise it at the time. Hospitals, school nurses and the smell of Cromesol were things which seemed to be a constant in our lives.

Above: A day out by Bluebird.

Left: A break for the bus men.

And first of all I want to get it out of my system and say hello to the very first school clinic nurse that I remember. Hello, you nameless sadist! There! I remember having an infection on my arm which was covered up by one of those big sticky fabric plasters which she 'wheeched' off in one go. It fairly brought tears to my eyes. Frankly she would have been first up against the wall…

Clinics were part of the new NHS system. We had one in William Street besides the nursery school. In institutional green, it was where the Green Ladies congregated: the district nurses. That's where we would be sent for minor ailments, for our BCG jabs or for having plasters ripped off mercilessly, and also for collecting the National Dried Milk (NDM) for baby siblings of my ilk.

For larger and more immediate threats to life there was the Yorkhill Children's Hospital. I remember it so well, with its higgledy-piggledy banks of wheelchairs ranged against the wall, the white-tiled waiting room and the hard tubular chairs. Of course I remember it well: I particularly treasure the long hours spent there after my big brother Martin threw a brush at me and it made a large hole in my forehead.

But my most favoured place in all the NHS was where Kathy Kirby worked. God knows what her name really was but she was a physiotherapist based in a converted church in Bath Street and I swear she was the image of lovely Kathy Kirby, the 1950s singer. If it had not been for her then I swear I would not have taken the foul and fiendish punishment meted out to my poor feet in the guise of treatment for flat feet.

Now in the 1950s, the expanding National Health Service needed premises and where better than churches which were no longer needed? This was the case for the physiotherapy chambers in Bath Street. I would arrive in the old church and go downstairs to an area of polished institutional brown lino and green cotton curtains. There I would be seated on a tubular metal chair in front of a massive cream-coloured electric machine covered with knobs and dials: if you think this sounds vaguely like a certain horror movie, you are heading in the right direction!

I then had to remove my socks and shoes and stick my feet into a plastic basin of hot water in which there were two flat aluminium electrodes. These had to be across the balls of my feet and across my heels. This being achieved, I was then electrocuted. Oh yes. They would start an electric current going through the electrodes, thus making my poor feet contract and theoretically improving the arches. The problem was that it wasn't always the same nurse and I dreaded a certain person who quite deliberately, it seemed to me, started the current too high so my feet would come flying out of the basin and the water would go skitting over the floor.

If that was not all uncomfortable enough, I think I had to bear this for a long time. It couldn't realistically have been longer than a half hour but the water began to get cold, the electricity got to feel just awful and I was sitting surrounded by curtains on my own thinking that I was going to be forgotten and my feet would shrivel up.

Anyway, it finished and then I was able to go upstairs to a sort of gym where Kathy Kirby taught me how to pick up marbles with my toes and caress my legs with my feet. It seems so long ago that I put up with all that torture and even cleaned my shoes and school uniform just to see Kathy.

I had previously forgotten that I also went to another clinic in the Garngad, Black Street Clinic, where I also walked on thin benches and played with tennis balls between my feet. And you know, I think all of this had absolutely no effect on my flat feet.

Incidentally, my daughter has the Meighan feet and to my surprise, astonishment and wonder, the only way they fix them now is to give the patient a customised plastic insert for their shoes. When I mentioned my treatment to my daughter's doctor, he was rather taken aback, saying that all those old remedies never worked and the modern thinking was for inserts. What was all that about then?

BONNIE SCOTLAND

BY BLUEBIRD

There is no better way of seeing the glories of Scotland—the bens, and glens, hills and heather than in the luxurious comfort of Alexanders 'BLUEBIRDS.' Anywhere you want to go in the North of Scotland—a fleet of over 1000 superb motor coaches at your disposal. Depots throughout Scotland, to assist your travel convenience to the fullest possible extent—and every bus a model of maintenance and equipment. Any time you wish, call and see one of our travel experts who will show you why it's better by 'BLUEBIRD.' Your holiday starts the moment you board the bus.

ALEXANDER'S
Bluebirds

Well, of course, I have suffered for my flat feet, possibly caused by excessive walking on forced marches throughout Glasgow. To top it off, my feet then were, according to general and informed opinion, rather large, being size eleven at age eleven. I think that this is probably an exaggeration, but you get the idea?

I wouldn't have minded except that, first of all, I was rather limited in the selection, being largely confined to Tuf industrial issues and Dunlop Green Flash tennis shoes (which I thought were rather snazzy myself). Secondly, the comments I endured – and this is a sad reflection on the creativity of the Glaswegian sarcastic, who could only suggest the one comment: 'Where do you buy your shoes. John Brown's?' But I've gotten over that. My style of footwear is rather polished now and not out of place among our present splay-footed youth (see page 86 for 'the birthplace of Michael's big shoes').

Talking of John Brown's, that reminds me of the ship designer who thought that Critical Path Analysis was a Greek ship owner! That reminds me of one of my other troubles about which I am not going to go into in any detail but what is known in our family as 'the Old Trouble'. Suffice it to say that it was confined to the nether regions. Being indisposed to the extent of frantic scratching I visited Doctor McGuire. He was quite reassuring in his way. His questioning of me ascertained that I had contracted this mystery disease through sitting on certain types of packing at the place where I had started an apprenticeship.

He was able to tell me with a straight face that he had recently been treating another patient with the same thing. On innocently asking how long the patient had had it the good doctor informed me that he had contracted it flying with Bomber Command during the Second Word War! Very interesting, and I am afraid, also very prophetic. At least it has caused a great deal of amusement to my family members!

I remember the smell of the first treatment that I got for my trouble. It was a watery purple liquid in one of those ribbed medicine bottles: 'not to be taken.' I had to apply this to my regions. But how? Well, after experimenting with cloths I discovered that the only thing that would work was by the application of the liquid to the parts by paint brush.

Unless one laid newspapers over a wide area it was impossible not to miss the parts and paint the town red. I had the difficult job of explaining to my mother why the bathroom mat was now various shades of purple. This was caused by: (a) my ineptitude in not standing in the bath or on a large rubber mat, (b) trying to get rid of the purple spots with a range of cleansing agents, some of which burned holes in the mat. And all the while there was me in the nude with a large purple bottom scrubbing wildly at the rapidly deteriorating mat. I cringe to think of it now, particularly as that particular topical application did not work. I went on to much scratchier things before relief was forthcoming. I have decided then that I am not going to tell you about the history of my warts. So there!

And by the way, many Glaswegians will know that Black Street (in a hushed whisper or guffaw depending on your condition) was where people (not me) went when they had diseases affecting their other regions. You know!

Now, if you think after reading the above, that I have a predisposition to casually condemn the National Health Service you are quite wrong. While it most certainly employed sadists like the aforementioned nurse, I have to tell you that in the 1950s, the NHS was in its infancy and like many other infants was feeling its way. In 1940 Glasgow had 5,190 cases of diphtheria, of which 226 were fatal. In 1955, as the result of a mass immunisation campaign, there were two cases and no fatalities. I was five by that time and while I remember the warning posters on the railings of my school, I do not remember anyone who was taken ill with diphtheria.

Within the space of a few weeks in the spring of 1957, 700,000 people in Glasgow came forward voluntarily to be screened against tuberculosis. The scourges of TB, diphtheria, scarlet fever, chicken pox, measles and polio seemed to be something that the population put up with prior to the 1950s and it is no mean feat that the NHS had accomplished so much in such a short time, making these diseases a thing of the past.

The birthplace of Michael's big shoes.

I do remember the starched but dedicated doctors and nurses who were able to accomplish then so much with so little. Why are things so difficult now and why do we take such a jaundiced view of the health services? Take cancer. While the big C is still feared, it is not so much now given the research and dedication of the medical profession, and those many volunteers who raise money for cancer research.

My Friend Pat

On this subject, I feel that I need to tell you a story about Pat Manning now. Pat was a very good friend of mine and lived, I think, in Dover Street or thereabouts. Our primary school class had ten Michaels, five Patricks, and about six others including one Freddy and one Roger. These last two were anomalies obviously, but nice fellows. The names overall would have given you an idea of the religion if you had not known.

Anyway, Pat was a big lad as I remember, rotund and red-headed and jolly. When I first met him at primary school I could see that from his ear to his cheek was a red rail track of about thirty stitches which slightly disfigured him. I do remember asking him about it and getting a vague reply.

I can't remember how much time we spent together but it seemed to me that whenever we did, Pat was very unfortunate. Pat was with us at school camp at Ballantrae and in the dormitory bed next to mine. I was prone in bed with an eye patch on and feeling miserable following a visit to a doctor after some fool had thrown a stick at me and hit me in the eye.

I remember so well that Pat had come running down the corridor to our dormitory only to see his hand appearing through a glass pane on the door, which had about twelve of these. The immediate effect was for spouts of blood to shoot out and I remember Mr Seenan, who was in charge of the trip, trying to stop the blood by applying pressure and a tourniquet. Pat was obviously off for a long time but came back to join us, pale and drawn with more stitches in his arm like a badge of courage.

Pat was also in the Scouts and that was probably were we spent most time together. In fact, when I remember it, we probably had lots of holidays then, for no sooner were we back from school camp, but we were off to Scout Camp, and on return from that, off on the family holiday to Girvan or 'Doon the Water' to Innellan or Dunoon.

Anyway, one of our Scout trips was to Jersey where we stayed at Sable d'Or which at that time was basically a field. Jersey is covered with remains of the German occupation during the Second World War. There are whole series of tunnels, and in the early 1960s there were still guns and turrets to be explored: anyway, I did so with Patrick – and down a dark tunnel in a gun emplacement poor Patrick fell and ended up on his jacksie, breaking his head and getting more stitches before reappearing much later at school.

Pat left school early, probably because his schooling had suffered so much. He got a job at the well-known sports shop Lumley's in Sauchiehall Street where I met him a couple of times probably when I was 'dogging' off from Stow College, just round the corner.

I lost touch with him and subsequently heard that Pat had died of leukaemia. Now this did not come as a surprise because for many years we had known, or at least I had known, that he had had the disease. All through these smaller problems he had fought against it and finally succumbed. It is a great regret of mine that I did not get to his funeral but this is for Pat. And I suppose that it is a good reminder of how good is our lot when we look at the stoicism and cheeriness of Pat Manning.

On a lighter note I remember the surgeon at the Glasgow Royal Infirmary who was operating: 'Scalpel!' 'Scalpel.' 'Swab.' 'Swab.' 'Scissors.' 'Scissors.' 'Forceps.' 'Whit?' 'Forceps!' 'Whit?' 'Where are you from, son?' 'Calton, sir.' 'Well, Tongs ya bass!'

Or the nurse who was looking for my friend who had been kept in hospital for a stomach operation and had been having three irrigations a day: he finally broke down and disappeared, to be found later having locked himself in a ward toilet. 'Are you there, Mr. Smith?' she said. 'Who goes there,' said he, 'friend or enema?' It was also he who thought that the Italian word for suppository was 'innuendo'.

Very recently I described to my daughter what a bread poultice was. It was used mainly for bringing boils to a head. But what did it smell like? Well it smelled like boiled bread!

My father certainly prepared them by heating white bread in water, placing it in a piece of flannel and applying it to the affected parts e.g. a large boil, while it was still hot. It was really sore! The supposed effect was to draw out the pus! (There's a good descriptive word). I can tell you that it was a bit weird going to bed with a soggy half-loaf bandaged to your bottom or other parts. It is very true that the 1950s was a time of great medical experimentation.

Reading

Once I had mastered 'Janet and John' I never looked back: I read till my eyes were sore. Again I have to look back and recognise the extent to which we were offered books in Glasgow. In the city centre there were any number of libraries and I had not understood the extent of this until I started to visit other parts of Great Britain and abroad. In North Street alone we were within walking distance of both Macintyre Street Library and the Mitchell Library.

Book stall, central Glasgow.

At these libraries you had free access and the number of books which could be borrowed was amazing, except that they were awfully strict if you didn't return them, even to the extent of coming to your door to demand the return of the books as well as fine you. Quite right!

Our school primary classes all had libraries and it was with eager anticipation that I waited for Friday afternoon when the library cupboard was open. I worked my way through most of Enid Blyton's 'Adventure' series, such as *The Castle of Adventure*. I devoured the Famous Five and moved on to John Buchan, Rider Haggard and *Kemlo, Space Cadet* as well as the brilliant science fiction stories of the Scottish writer, Angus MacVicar, such as *Return to the Lost Planet*.

We took books everywhere including hospitals and clinics. I should tell you that in those days our waiting times were not measured in months and years but in hours, but those hours came all at the one time and your heart sank when you turned up at the eye pavilion to find a queue of about fifty in front of you. At least you had a book and the latest edition of *The Eagle* with Dan Dare, or *The Hotspur*.

I read when I shouldn't; keeping books in my desk to read when the teacher wasn't looking. I read under the covers and I read anything that I could get my hands on. Now here is a confession: while I was staying at my Auntie Peggy's for a few days I ran out of books and comics to read. The problem was that my cousins are all girls so the only reading to hand was the *Bunty*, *Girl's Own* and *The Head Girl of the Chalet School* by Eleanor Brent Dyer: I have to confess now that I quite liked it but nothing would have dragged it out of me then.

Football

I had intended not to say anything about football because I knew little about it then and know as little about it now. While it is was worthwhile hobby for those who played it and a pastime of sorts for those who watched it, I could not understand the undignified obsession that affected and still affects even very sensible graduates of esteemed academic institutions, many of them part of my extended family.

Well here we are then, saying something about football and I suppose in writing a book about Glasgow sights and smells, how could I ignore 'The Beautiful Game'?

Football was a way of life in Glasgow and in Anderston. It was inseparable from church and inseparable from school. It was the starting point in discussions in taxis, bars, buses, queues and the barber shop. The problem is that if you knew very little about football you were put in the unenviable position of appearing a bit odd if you were in the barber's chair and asked what you thought of that goal in the last minute.

Anyway, I didn't have the memory for football statistics and you would really have to be motivated to want to learn the names, colours and nicknames of every team, not only in the four Scottish divisions but in all the English divisions as well.

I am talking here about my older brother, Martin, who was able to do this, no doubt with a view to answering questions about it in future pub quizzes. Getting the *Topical Times* was obviously a help to him while I preferred my *Eagle Annual* at Christmas.

You may recognise a certain cynicism creeping into my attitude towards football. Not so. I have learned to value my many forced trips in black and white to places such as Shawfield to see Celtic play Clyde, Kilmarnock or Airdrie for Airdrieonians. Also I am able to talk honourably about seeing Celtic playing the famous Third Lanark at Queen's Park, or St Mirren beating Celtic in the 1959 Scottish Cup final in Paisley. Irrespective of the fact that I hardly remember anything that happened as: (a) I wasn't interested and would more likely wander round the backs of the stands which generally weren't very interesting or (b) because I was a four-eyed specky bastard (FESB). That was a fairly normal description of someone who wore glasses when I was but a boy. These days it may come under some discriminatory legislation but then it was par for the course. And as I was that specky bastard I could hardly see who was on the pitch, never mind remember their names as well as their numbers. On the following page is a fine example of a FESB from the 1950s in Glasgow. To be honest he looks just as I did then! But I think that these are Glasgow High School boys who went to posh school and wore jobby coloured jackets (see page 91).

Talking of the smell of the crowd and the roar of the greasepaint, well the combined smells of many thousands of men at Hampden was pretty overpowering. Besides the smell of bodies you had to contend with going to the toilet. I suppose 'toilet' was a rather elevated word for what were really cement walls at the end of which lines of men would queue to get rid of their McEwan's or Mick Jagger.

Some of the grounds had the real brick shithouses, as in 'built like one', all brick and concrete roofs. Unfortunately, the small windows and slot-like doors had the effect of containing within the edifice the combined smells of many thousands letting loose. Believe me, the smell was overpowering and, on a cold day, you could see the steam from the pee pouring through the windows. Is this really low writing? Please let me know.

Of course, in those early days before family outings, there were no women's toilets and there was a procedure to be followed in this case. When a woman needed to use the facilities then help was sought from male friends who would bar the entrance to the loo to prevent men going in while the lady went about her business: this, of course, often provoked irritation in the needy.

Of course, you didn't really need to go to the loo. What would happen on many occasions would be that a chap would point his mechanism at the end of an empty beer can that had been properly torn asunder with the aid of the triangular-ended can opener used in those days, sometimes also as a weapon (the can-opener I mean).

Woe betide the poor aimer who hadn't alerted his fellows to the imminence of his action as he might spray them in a very ungentlemanly fashion and this again might create an altercation. Or he might be nudged and therefore catch his thingy on the sharp edge of the torn can. 'I cut myself peeing?'

Of course, in those days, the terraces were really just fields kept together with lengths of wood which would keep the earth back, one higher than the next. When a chap had finished using his Tennent's can for the aforesaid purpose, well he would generally place it on the edge of the plank where, inevitably, when Celtic scored, the can would be propelled onto the ground to splash on feet and create ponds and rivulets of pee. It should be said that the more exciting a match the more you were apt to leave the ground with soggy boots. It has also been pointed out by a poor Partick Thistle supporter, my friend Henry, that some of the said fans dispensed with the need for the can. 'Hey, you want a hot leg pal?'

While we are mentioning the smells of urine mixed with the earthy smell of the terraces, we might also mention that these cannot be separated from the smell of hot Bovril along with the other meaty smell of hot pies. These would be sold from huts at the back of the stands to all and sundry including those who had not had the opportunity to wash their hands after partaking of the aforesaid relief operation. Not that they might wash their hands, for there was not the opportunity to do so given the absence of ablutionary facilities. Given the doubtful hygiene practices it is a wonder that scores of people did not come down with food poisoning, or maybe they did.

Now to the subject of Subbuteo – I never ever got used to the idea of Subbuteo. Let me explain: Subbuteo is and was a game played with models of footballers, all about an inch high standing on little plastic wobbly things on which they could rock backwards and forwards. These were available in all league colours and you could decide whether Celtic was to play Chelsea at home or away.

Of course, whether football is full-scale, miniaturised or sub-miniature, in the case of Subbuteo, you still needed expanded areas of real estate in which to play it. The former was no problem as there were more brokies and back courts than you could shake a stick at. The problem with miniaturised footie, that is, one-to-one played with a tanner ba, rolled up sock or such other ba,

A fine example of a FESB in 1950s Glasgow (front, centre).

was that, in inclement weather or on winter's evenings, my brother's choice of Hampden Park tended to be the kitchen or the shared bedroom where the rest of us were trying to do other things such as sleep, study or just be. This conflict of purpose inevitably brought arguments, if not full-scale war.

What better place, I suppose, than to play right in front of the fire with complete and utter disregard for anyone who happened to want heat or maybe just to get past. The flicking of the little men was also accompanied by crowd noises and Hampden roars that my brothers got very good at. But just like playing Monopoly or Ludo, good things had to come to an end and this was either through the accusations of cheating, crushing a footballer to a little footballer death or standing on the goals.

It got really quite ridiculous, to the extent that visiting chums would bring their own teams, stands and little battery-powered floodlights which put the hems on the rest of us doing anything. The darkness and the need to make pots of tea of course resulted in broken footballers and more kitchen conflict. At least none of it was sectarian. To this day while I have no problem with the tribalism inherent in football and while I can understand the manly comradeship that it instils, I still can't get enthused except for the big games.

This all reminds me of the friend of mine, a Glasgow Celtic fan who was in America on holiday. While he was travelling he was told of an old Indian who had the most amazing and fantastic memory. He decided that he would put this to the test. He travelled by car to the Indian Reservation, had to trek for a day on pony and then walked for five hours before he came to the Indian village. He was pointed in the direction of an old tepee. He walked in to see in the dark, musty smoky atmosphere an old Indian squatting on the ground. He explained to the Indian what he had come for and the Indian said, 'just ask', so he asked, 'who won the Scottish cup in 1951?' 'Celtic beat Motherwell 1-0,' he replied.

An incident from a kitchen game between brothers.

Amazed, he thanked the Indian and stumbled out and told this story many times in Morrison's bar. However, Glaswegians are true cynics and rarely believed him.

Ten years later he found himself back in the same area of America and wondered if the old Indian was still there. This time he hired a light aircraft and then was able to walk only two hours to the village. To his amazement he found that the Indian was still there, sitting in his old tepee. 'This'll get him', he thought as he wondered about another question. 'McPhail in the thirteenth minute,' said the Indian before he could ask.

(The above took me some time to research in order to make sure that I got my facts right so that the older supporters sitting in Glasgow bars couldn't challenge it. I told the story to my brother Martin, he of the *Topical Times*. 'Aye, but which McPhail was it?' he said. 'There were two!' Ye cannae win.

New Smells, New Beginnings

You will find very little in here of the 'No Mean City' variety and I can be easily accused of sentimentalising Glasgow, because I haven't dwelt on the violence or the poverty or the dirt of the 1950s in Glasgow, and in particular in Anderston.

That's very probably because I saw very little of this even though I was brought up in the very centre of the city between 1950 and 1965. Neither was I sheltered. Very specifically when I was about twelve I got a doing from two Castlemilk nyaffs when me and Charlie were doing our Cub hiking badge. Not only did they take our bus fares home, they took our Mars Bars and left us with only our gas-mask bags and black eyes! (In those days gas-mask bags were real cool to carry school books and stuff.)

The city centre was not a frightening place. Yes, there were murders, and maybe I was lucky, but I wandered the streets and lanes of Glasgow without a worry. Yes, there were sometimes incidents that I remember but they were never to cause a lasting impression that Glasgow was a violent place to be.

Yes, people took a drink but the pubs and drunks were generally well managed by professional bar staff like my Uncle Jimmy. The police were more in evidence and more likely to know the troublemakers and they were very quick on the scene when there was trouble, as in the incident at St Pat's when I kicked the policeman. But that was minor and all part of the fun

People were more self-reliant then and certainly slimmer although few people went hungry. Education was treated with respect if not with awe as that was the only way out and up if that's what you wanted. But it all changed and some of it had to change. But it changed too much.

I wasn't aware of the Bruce Plan when I was growing up in Anderston in the 1950s. I did not appreciate the scale of the changes proposed for us in Anderston, The Gorbals, Cowcaddens and many other city areas. For there were plans afoot to demolish large swathes of the city to be replaced by regulated city blocks for 'community living' as well as high-speed routes for the motor car. What a relief that it didn't happen. 'What do you mean, didn't happen?' I hear you shout with one voice. 'Of course it did. Just look at what happened in The Gorbals, the motorway, the Kingston Bridge, Easterhouse etc.'

When I say 'didn't happen', I mean that all of the plans didn't happen. What did happen was only a very small part of what was actually intended. What was intended was also the loss of what now remains of other parts of old Glasgow. There was even talk of Glasgow Cathedral and the Necropolis going, as would the Glasgow School of Art have done! If you think what has happened has been criminal then, for you, the Bruce Plan would have been akin to architectural and social mass murder.

My first memories of the 'Clearances' was the removal of the bodies from our local cemetery to Linn Park, the gradual and then frenetic removal of buildings with massive balls on chains, mechanical shovels and bulldozers and lorries just like Stanley Baker in T*he Hell Drivers*.

The destruction of our homes and lives was total and complete and the smell of it was everywhere. Like death, the odour of collapsed tenements was both pervasive and memorable. It was of old damp plaster and lathe, ancient mortar and rotting wood combined.

The copper and lead pipes had already been stripped, as had the lead off the roofs. Where water had not been turned off, fountains spurted from mounds of rubble or from the sides of buildings cascading onto the ground below.

Boarded-up shops where you had bought sweeties were broken into for fun and profit. Everywhere, windows were broken and corrugated iron was going up.

While everything else went for landfill, the doors, still with handles attached became makeshift site walls or were whisked away to become gang huts. As the walls came down, lives were exposed, the taste in wallpaper, even pictures left on walls, a testament to the hurried evacuation to Castlemilk, Easterhouse and 'the Drum', Drumchapel.

We had moved to Knightswood but, despite the new adventures there, our lives – Scouts, Guides, Cubs, Boys' Brigade, youth club, altar boys – were still in Anderston and we would, for a time, cling on to these as on to a raft in uncertain social waters. For me, Knightswood was a leafy suburban glade with suburban-type neighbours. It was a different again Glasgow and one to grow into. It was almost akin to those areas we called 'spam belts' or where they wore fur coats and nae knickers! Or where they insisted on giving their children Christian names that should have been surnames. For instance, in our class at school we had a chum from the Mulgay (or pronounced Milngavie with a jorrie in the mooth). To this day I don't know if he was called Cameron Campbell or Campbell Cameron.

Shamrock St Dan Ferguson.

I went back and visited our old building in North Street. A wall of corrugated iron barred the close but I got in through the back door and wandered the stairs. How quickly the smell of death had claimed the old place. I stood in our bedroom. I see it still now, looking up Argyle Street, already with far fewer cars than there had been before. It was dying.

I climbed to the top of our flat roof for a last look over the roofs and to where I had seen the long ladders fall on that terrible night on Cheapside Street.

Lastly I visited Doctor MacGuire's surgery and it was as if he was still there and I was the last patient, sitting on the old black horse hair couch below the print of 'The Anatomist'. Everything was there as if he had just walked out, most amazingly, the old medicines, the moulds for pills, the wooden and Victorian instruments, the furniture and the lovely engraved panel on the front door.

For many years I kept two souvenirs, two blue and white ceramic jars marked 'opii'. I left through the corrugated-iron front door. I was filthy and a bit sad. I caught the bus home and never went back.

I had not appreciated the changes to come. I vaguely knew of Castlemilk, where I got my 'doing' and the other 'schemes'. I remember on one of our walks my father pointing to a drawing on a poster of the proposed new Basil Spence 'High-Rise flats' in the Gorbals. These were to be state-of-the-art living towers and at each end of each level of the long grey concrete buildings were to be hanging gardens!

I since wondered how Sir Basil imagined how the typical Gorbalian was going to carry a hundredweight of No. 1 Sphagnum Peat Moss to the top of the block when the lifts were broken, as they turned out very often to be. Maybe he was thinking of opening a garden centre at the top where the residents could more easily steal the product.

Anyway it's gone now, blown up, and may the monstrosity rest in peace. Many of the remaining monuments to stupidity are gone or have been renovated and turned into something less intimidating. However, the roads were to get bigger but the Bruce Plan was downgraded in the nick of time. We are left with the motorway smells and sound through my heartland and, at Anderston Cross, simply the memory of a smell.

PUBLIC SCHOOL

Session 19 _59_ 19 _60_

CLASS _V 2_

PRIZE

Awarded to

Michael Meighan

FOR

GENERAL EXCELLENCE

_____ HEAD TEACHER.

R. Stewart Macintosh

DIRECTOR OF EDUCATION

EDUCATION DEPARTMENT, CORPORATION OF GLASGOW.

Just the best! 'That's yer time now please.'

Other local titles published by Tempus

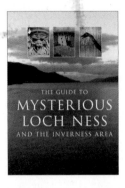

The Guide to Mysterious Loch Ness and the Inverness Area
GEOFF HOLDER

This is a guide to everything supernatural, paranormal, folkloric, eccentric and, above all, mysterious that has occurred on the dark waters of Loch Ness and the surrounding area of Inverness. Containing fairies and martyrs, telepathy, exorcism and magic, druids, witches, mermaids, demons and saints (and based on texts both ancient and modern), it is a fascinating introduction to the heritage of this enigmatic area.

978 07524 4485 7

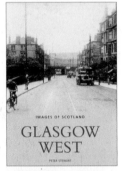

Glasgow West
DR PETER STEWART

This fascinating collection of more than 220 archive images, many never published, explores the history of the west of Glasgow over the last 150 years. Much has changed over that time, but many of the area's Victorian and Edwardian terraces retained their grandeur as fashions and faces evolved around them. This nostalgic volume will delight anyone who has lived or worked in the west of Glasgow and provides a valuable social record of the way things were in this thriving city.

978 07524 3658 6

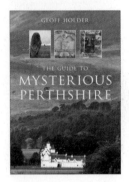

The Guide to Mysterious Perthshire
GEOFF HOLDER

A comprehensive guide to everything folkloric, supernatural, paranormal, eccentric and odd that has been recorded about the area, Mysterious Perthshire provides a fascinating introduction to the tombstones, simulacra, standing stones, gargoyles and archaeological curiosities of Perthshire. Included are tales of ghosts, fairies, witchcraft, freak weather, strange deaths and hoaxes, making it the ideal guide for armchair adventurers and on-location visitors alike.

978 07524 4140 5

Glasgow East
GORDON ADAMS

This book contains more than 200 archive images of the east of Glasgow. From images of mills, miners, weavers, breweries and, of course, brewers, to beautiful buildings (and sprawling tenements), inns, picture palaces and skating rinks, this is a celebration of the city's heritage and the lives of its inhabitants – a rare and nostalgic glimpse of life in the area as it used to be.

978 07524 4567 0

If you are interested in purchasing other books published by Tempus, or in case you have difficulty finding any Tempus books in your local bookshop, you can also place orders directly through our website

www.tempus-publishing.com